CAREER WRITING SKILLS

CAREER WRITING SKILLS

Judith Mallegol Cardanha
Educational Consultant

GLENCOE
McGraw-Hill

New York, New York
Columbus, Ohio
Mission Hills, California
Peoria, Illinois

Printed in the United States of America.

Send all inquiries to:
Glencoe/McGraw-Hill
936 Eastwind Drive
Westerville, OH 43081

ISBN 0-256-13835-4

2 3 4 5 6 7 8 9 10   073   04 03 02 01 00 99 98 97

Preface

Career Writing Skills is a book for everyone who needs to write. Whether it be to write a letter complaining about a defective copy machine or inquiring about a job opening, to complete a job or credit-card application, or to compose an invitation to an office party, everyone needs to be competent in and to feel comfortable with the English language.

Career Writing Skills takes any career student from an understanding of the kinds of words, through constructing the four kinds of sentences, to writing a basic paragraph and applying that to the various types of writing a person may encounter in the career world. Nothing creates a poorer impression in the business world than bad spelling and grammar. The student is alerted to commonly made mistakes in spelling, grammar, and sentence structure and is given ample practice to reinforce positive skills.

All sentences and examples are career related. They will appeal to students in all career fields and should give them guidelines for their own work.

♦ Benefits of This Book

Students who use this text-workbook will receive a thorough course in English grammar. They will review parts of speech, parts of sentences, punctuation, noun and pronoun cases, verb tenses, agreement within a sentence, and so on. All this will be done with examples and practice exercises relating to careers.

Students will learn to recognize mistakes in grammar, spelling, and sentence construction so they can avoid them in their own writing.

Students will learn to recognize positive elements and good structure in paragraphs so they can model their own writings on them.

Students will learn to write everything from a memo to a résumé to prepare them for many of the writing forms they might meet in their careers.

♦ Skills to Be Learned

Grammar Skills

Students will learn to:

Identify the parts of speech and use them correctly.

Use the correct cases of nouns and pronouns.

Form the correct tenses of regular and irregular verbs and use them correctly.

Identify the parts of a sentence and form them correctly.

Use correct punctuation.

Writing Skills

Students will learn to:

Form sentences.

Have proper agreement of subjects and predicates.

Identify and use the four kinds of sentences.

Identify the main idea and other kinds of sentences in a paragraph.

Proofread a paragraph for grammar, spelling, and punctuation.

Edit a paragraph for sequence and clarity of thought.

Write letters, memos, invitations, and résumés; fill out forms; and take messages.

◆ Users of *Career Writing Skills*

Career Writing Skills has been written for career students of all ages who want to improve their writing skills. In difficult economic times, many jobs are eliminated, and people who have been working for many years find themselves training for new careers. Students just out of high school know that the job market is tight and want the edge that they can get from training in a career school.

Using correct grammar, punctuation, and spelling are skills that make anyone a more valuable employee. When a worker knows that he or she possesses good basic writing skills, then that person is going to be more confident and will do a better job at any writing task he or she undertakes.

Whether students feel that they are weak in some areas of writing or just need a good review, *Career Writing Skills* will strengthen their skills and reinforce what they already know while filling any gaps that might exist in their knowledge.

◆ Learning Features

Lesson titles are straightforward indications of what is presented in the lesson.

Objectives for each lesson appear right after the title to focus both the instructor and the student on the goal(s) of the lesson.

Key terms appear in italic type and also in boldface type in formal definitions when appropriate.

Examples illustrate the concepts being taught.

Boxed numerals indicate steps in a procedure and give students a definite plan of attack for whatever the word skill is.

Lists of examples of parts of speech, verb forms, difficult words, and so on, appear throughout the book to give the student easy reference materials.

Practice exercises, with one or more exercises already answered, give the student a chance to practice the learned concepts in career-related sentences.

Answer Key in its entirety appears at the back of the book so students can immediately check their work or so the book can be used in a self-teaching manner. The pages are perforated so the instructor can remove them if the students are not to have them.

Supplementary Exercises, Cumulative Reviews, Chapter Tests, and a *Final Exam* appear in the Instructor's Manual.

The *Instructor's Manual* contains Lesson Objectives along with plans for each lesson and a flowchart illustrating how the program can be implemented in 36-hour and 24-hour courses. It also contains the Answer Key.

Acknowledgments

I am very grateful to Carol Long, my executive editor, who believed in me and in this book, and to Anna Drake, my developmental editor, for her many suggestions and for keeping me on track. And a good deal of credit for this book goes to the many grammar and writing teachers I have had over the years, as well as the example of the many authors with whom I have worked. Thanks to my typists, Madeline Brewster and Diane Drake, and to the editors and designers who put the final product together.

The comments, observations, and suggestions of the following reviewers were of great help in developing the manuscript.

Mary C. M. Anderson	DeVry Institute
Jane Ann O. Benson	Southern Ohio College
Kirk W. Bromley	P.S.I. Institute
Kathy Grimes	Trend College
Beth A. Tarquino	Bryant & Stratton
Linda C. Werner	Trend College

Judith Mallegol Cardanha

To the Student

Language allows you to share thoughts in three ways: by speaking, by reading, and by writing. Like most people, you were probably able to speak before you could read or write. The order of the next steps—reading and writing—depended on your individual talents.

Reading and writing go together—you write something and someone else reads what you have written, and vice versa. The message you wish to share with someone may be very clear in your head. However, if you cannot transfer those clear thoughts into clear writing, you will not be able to share those thoughts with your reader.

Career Writing Skills will begin with the kinds of words that are the basis of any writing—nouns, verbs, conjunctions, and so on. You will be shown the correct way to assemble the words into sentences and the best way to join sentences into the various forms of writing that you might be required to use in your career—memos, letters, messages, invitations, and so on.

Two important writing skills are proofreading and editing. You will be shown instances of common mistakes in, for example, spelling, punctuation, and grammar. You will also be shown how to mark mistakes and corrections so that the material can be rewritten properly.

You may already be familiar with some of the lessons in this book. Take this opportunity to reinforce what you already know and to learn and improve other skills. Remember that people write in different styles. Whatever your style, you must use language in a clear and correct way.

Contents

CAREER WRITING SKILLS

Parts of Speech

Nouns

Objective   To identify and use a noun.

A **noun** is a word that names a person, place, or thing.

Person	Place	Thing
woman	office	computer
boss	hospital	stapler
clerk	station	loyalty (nouns can be an idea or a feeling)
hostess	shop	thermometer
plumber	bank	wrench

The above nouns are *common nouns*. They name ordinary persons, places, or things.

Nouns that name particular persons, places, or things are called *proper nouns*. They begin with a capital letter.

These nouns are *proper nouns*.

Person	Place	Thing
Mr. Waverly	Paris	Empire State Building
Ms. Clark	New York	Golden Gate Bridge
Dr. Cerone	California	White House
George Washington	Mars	Grand Canyon

You know a word is a noun if it names a person, place, or thing.

A *compound noun* is a noun that is made up of two or more words and considered as one word. Some compound nouns are called "open compounds"—*disk drive* is an open compound—it is two words with a space between them. Other compound nouns are called "closed compounds"—*president-elect* and *airplane* are closed compounds—each is two words with either a hyphen or no space at all between them. (Note: Compounds can be formed by more than two words.)

Open Compound	Closed Compound
master builder	dogcatcher
decision making	clearinghouse
notary public	bookkeeping
money order	masterpiece
pipe fitter	self-confidence
common stock	checkbook
blood test	commander-in-chief

EXAMPLE

Underline all nouns in this sentence.

Janet took his temperature and blood pressure.

1 Read the sentence.

2 Look at each word and decide if it is a noun.

Janet?	Yes, a person.
took?	No.
his?	No.
temperature?	Yes, a thing.

and?	No.
blood pressure?	Yes, a thing.

<u>Janet</u> took his <u>temperature</u> and <u>blood pressure</u>.

PRACTICE

Underline all nouns in each sentence. The first one is done for you.

1. We attended a <u>conference</u> in <u>Canada</u>.
2. My boss sent out a memo on being on time.
3. The restaurant had 14 tables for two people and 10 tables for four people.
4. Malcolm took two hours for lunch.
5. Sherry is a good receptionist because she likes people.
6. The repairman said the condenser in the refrigerator was no good.
7. The caterer forgot to bring the tablecloths.
8. Many tourists like to shop in Mexico.
9. The judge asked the stenographer to read the last statement.
10. There are many jobs for secretaries in Washington, D.C.

LESSON 1.2

Singular and Plural Nouns

Objective   To identify and give the correct form of singular and plural nouns.

A noun can name one person, place, or thing. Then it is a *singular* noun. A noun can name persons, places, and things. Then it is a *plural* noun.

Whether a noun is singular or plural is the *number* of the noun.

Singular	Plural
typist—one person	typists—more than one person
city—one place	cities—more than one place
desk—one thing	desks—more than one thing

Note that most plurals are formed by adding -s to the singular form.

typist   —   typists
desk   —   desks

The plural of *city* is *cities*. That is an *irregular* plural. (Irregular plurals are covered in the next lesson.)

Write the plural of each noun. The first one is done for you.

1. hospital   _____hospitals_____   2. floor   _____

3. pencil   _____   4. pipe   _____

5. order   _____   6. sample   _____

7. monitor   _____   8. invoice   _____

9. job   _____   10. technician   _____

Write the singular of each noun. The first one is done for you.

11. pens   _____pen_____   12. uniforms   _____

13. blanks   _____   14. calls   _____

15. machines   _____   16. raises   _____

17. sales   _____   18. brakes   _____

19. computers   _____   20. papers   _____

Choose the correct form of the noun and underline it. The first one is done for you.

21. My (client, clients) each want to be first.

22. (Sale, Sales) are up this week.

23. The technician took a (sample, samples) of my blood.

24. Six (floor, floors) of that building are occupied by my firm.

25. The mechanic said that my car's (transmission, transmissions) needs to be overhauled.

26. I had to buy a new (keyboard, keyboards) for my computer.

27. Nursing jobs often mean working on different (shift, shifts).

28. My boss is glad when I can give him a good (idea, ideas).

29. Samantha sent (résumé, résumés) to 20 companies.

30. It is very annoying to a dental assistant if a patient is late for an (appointment, appointments).

Irregular Plurals

Objective   To form the plurals of irregular nouns.

In Lesson 1.2, you saw that the plural of *city* is *cities*. The plural of *city* is not formed by simply adding *-s* to *city*.

This lesson explains how to form the plural of irregular nouns—the groups of nouns that form the plural in a different way.

> The letters of the alphabet can be classified as vowels or consonants.
>
> vowels—a, e, i, o, u
> consonants—all other letters

1. Nouns that end in *y:*
   If the letter before the *y* is a consonant (not a vowel), change the *y* to *i* and add *-es*.

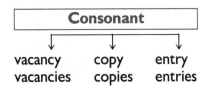

   If the letter before the *y* is a vowel, add *-s* to form the plural in the usual way.

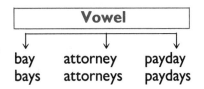

2. Nouns that end in *s, x, zz, sh,* or *ch,* add *-es* to the singular.

buzz	batch	tax	boss	dish
buzzes	batches	taxes	bosses	dishes

3. Nouns that end in *o*:
   If the letter before the *o* is a vowel or if the word refers to music, add *-s* to the singular.

Music		Vowel	
piano	alto	radio	portfolio
pianos	altos	radios	portfolios

If the letter before the *o* is a consonant, sometimes *-es* is added to the singular.

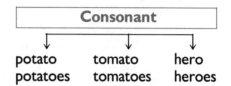

Consonant		
potato	tomato	hero
potatoes	tomatoes	heroes

But:

zero	taco	memo
zeros	tacos	memos

4. Nouns that end in *f* or *fe:*
   Most change the *f* or *fe* to *ve* and add *-s*.

shelf	wharf	life	loaf
shelves	wharves	lives	loaves

   All words that end in *ff* and some that end in *f* or *fe* just add *-s* to the singular.

staff	chef	safe	chief
staffs	chefs	safes	chiefs

5. Some words have unusual plurals, and you just have to remember them.

man	woman	child	mouse	goose
men	women	children	mice	geese
ox	alumnus	bacterium	tooth	
oxen	alumni	bacteria	teeth	

6. Some words are the same in singular and plural.

   aircraft   fish   series   deer   sheep

7. Some words are always singular.

   arithmetic   air conditioning   self-confidence

8. Some words look like a plural but are singular.

   economics   mathematics   mumps   thanks

9. In compound nouns, the main word is made plural.

notary public		master builder
notari<u>es</u> public	*but*	master builder<u>s</u>
vice president		attorney-at-law
vice president<u>s</u>	*but*	attorney<u>s</u>-at-law
checkbook		passerby
checkbook<u>s</u>	*but*	passer<u>s</u>by

PRACTICE

Write the plural of each noun. The first one is done for you.

1. reply   <u>replies</u>
2. solo
3. leaf
4. commander-in-chief
5. alloy
6. emergency
7. boss
8. finish
9. café
10. stitch
11. series
12. dictionary
13. certified public accountant
14. brain wave
15. waitress
16. video
17. box
18. repairman
19. half
20. data processor

Possessive Form of Nouns

Objective   To recognize and form the possessive of nouns.

A **possessive noun** shows ownership.

The possessive form is shown by *'s* or *s'* added to a noun. (The ' is called an *apostrophe*.) Ownership can also be shown by a phrase beginning with the word *of*. Rewriting the sentence to use an *of* phrase can be a check to see if the possessive form is correct. Change the possessive to an *of* phrase and see if it makes sense.

EXAMPLE

car's exhaust system	exhaust system of the car
manual's cover	cover of the manual
computers' manufacturer	manufacturer of the computers
companies' pension plans	pension plans of the companies
Mike's résumé	résumé of Mike
Browns' competition	competition of the Browns

A possessive noun can be singular or plural. To decide if a possessive noun is singular or plural, look at the part of the word before the apostrophe.

EXAMPLE

Singular	Plural
car's	*computers'*
manual's	*companies'*
Mike's	*Browns'*

♦ Rules for Forming Possessives

1. Singular nouns form the possessive by adding *'s*. *But:* If a singular proper noun has more than one syllable and ends in *s, x,* or *z,* just add the apostrophe. (This is done so that the possessive form is not awkward to pronounce.)

Alex' desk

Ms. Diaz' office

the Phillips' business

2. Plural nouns that end in *s* form the possessive by adding just the apostrophe. If the plural does not end in *s*, add *'s*.

Regular Plural Possessive	Irregular Plural Possessive
pencils'	children's
menus'	feet's
freezers'	bacteria's
assistants'	attorneys-at-law's
Mendeyes'	alumni's
Barkers'	people's

3. Compound modifiers form the possessive depending on the meaning of the phrase.

''Tony and Ann's business'' means ''the business belonging to (both) Tony and Ann.''

''Tony's and Ann's businesses'' means ''the business that belongs to Tony and the business that belongs to Ann.''

PRACTICE

Change the *of* phrase to the possessive form. The first one is done for you.

1. keyboard of the computer   the computer's keyboard
2. secretary of Maria   _____
3. calculator of the accountant   _____
4. tools of the welders   _____
5. samples of the salespeople   _____
6. recipes of the chef   _____
7. uniform of the nurse   _____
8. reputation of the lab technician   _____
9. rooms of the hotel   _____
10. assistant of the administrator   _____

Put the apostrophe in the correct place. The first one is done for you.

11. the s h i p's officer
12. the d o c t o r s office
13. the s e c r e t a r i e s desks
14. the p a t i e n t s rooms
15. her c a r s bumper
16. those p r i n t e r s ribbons
17. the p l u m b e r s van
18. his r o o m s air conditioner
19. the b u i l d i n g s elevator
20. the w o m e n s experiences

LESSON 1.5

Personal Pronouns

Objective   To understand pronouns and to use personal pronouns correctly.

> A **pronoun** is a word that takes the place of a noun or a group of words.

You use pronouns in your speech and writing all the time because they let you avoid repeating nouns.

EXAMPLE

Suppose your name is Leah. Without pronouns, you would write something like the following:

Leah's sister and Leah work for Leah's sister's and Leah's father.

A pronoun can be used for each underlined portion of the sentence.

My sister and I work for our father.

Pronouns have person and number, and singular pronouns have gender. *Person* can be:

first person—*speaker*—I, me, my, mine, we, us, our, ours

second person—*spoken to*—you, your, yours

third person—*spoken about*—he, him, his, she, her, hers, it, its,
they, them, their, theirs

Number can be:

> singular—I, me, mine, you, yours, he, him, his, she, her, hers, it, its

> plural—we, us, our, ours, your, yours, they, them, their, theirs

Gender can be:

> masculine: he, him, his

> feminine: she, her, hers

> neuter: it, it, its

This can be summarized in a chart:

	1st Person	2nd Person	3rd Person	
Singular	I, me, my, mine	you, your, yours	masculine feminine neuter	he, him, his she, her, hers it, its
Plural	we, us, our, ours	you, your, yours	masculine feminine and neuter	they, them, their, theirs

EXAMPLE

Underline the pronouns in this sentence.

> Brad met his new boss at our house.

1   Read the entire sentence.

2   Look at each word, and decide if it is a pronoun.

Brad?	No, proper noun.
met?	No.
his?	Yes, so underline.
new?	No.
boss?	No, common noun.
at?	No.
our?	Yes, so underline.
house?	No, common noun.

Brad met <u>his</u> new boss at <u>our</u> house.

PRACTICE

Underline the pronouns in each sentence. The first one is done for you.

1. Can <u>you</u> ship that report to <u>me</u> today?
2. Mr. Fasco told his employees that they should let him know about any problems.
3. I want to tell you about the raise I am getting.
4. She wanted to have her résumé printed on ivory paper.
5. They sent him to the emergency room to have his eye checked.
6. The salesperson helped me pick out my new word-processing program.
7. They were very happy with the hotel that the travel agent had recommended to them.
8. He hoped that his experience would get him a better job at the new auto-body shop.
9. Our health insurance is better than theirs.
10. We made an appointment to tour their new printing plant.

LESSON 1.6

Agreement of Pronouns

Objective   To make pronouns agree with antecedents.

As you learned in the last lesson, a pronoun takes the place of a noun. A pronoun takes the place of a *particular* noun, so the reader will not be confused as to what the pronoun is referring.

Confusing:	Alfonso sold Mark his computer.
	Does ''his'' refer to ''Alfonso'' or ''Mark''?
	You cannot tell.
Clear:	Alfonso sold his computer to Mark.
	''his'' refers to ''Alfonso''—the computer was Alfonso's.

The noun to which a pronoun refers is its *antecedent*. ''Alfonso'' is the antecedent of ''his.''

The pronoun must *agree* with its antecedent in person, number, and gender.

Person:	''Alfonso'' is third person—''his'' is third person.
Number:	''Alfonso'' is singular—''his'' is singular.
Gender:	''Alfonso'' is masculine—''his'' is masculine.

EXAMPLE

Draw an arrow from the pronoun to the antecedent.

Anna's boss called her on the intercom.

EXAMPLE

Choose the correct pronoun.

Ms. Walsh and Ms. Klein took a refresher course to improve (their, her) word-processing skills.

- The pronouns refer to whoever took the refresher course.
- Ms. Walsh *and* Ms. Klein took the refresher course.
- Ms. Walsh *and* Ms. Klein   { third person / plural / feminine
- *their* is the correct pronoun.

PRACTICE

Underline the correct pronouns. Then draw an arrow from the pronoun to its antecedent. The first one is done for you.

1. Luis and (his, its) boss attended a conference.
2. Cathy left (her, his) job for a better-paying one.
3. When the power went off, Tom lost all the data (he, him) had taken six hours to input.
4. The accountant sent them (their, her) tax forms to sign.
5. Vanessa, you should check the schedule for (your, his) hours for next week.
6. The dental technician told Aaron that (he, they) should floss more often.
7. The staff on the cruise ship did everything (she, they) could to make the guests comfortable.
8. That auto-body shop is known for (its, her) honesty.
9. Sandy is hoping to have (their, her) associate's degree in two months.
10. By working through a temporary agency, Janelle added to (her, his) list of experiences.

LESSON 1.7

Verbs

Objective   To identify and use verbs.

A **verb** is a word that expresses action or state of being.

Action means "doing something." Here are some action verbs.

write	repair	sell	call
shop	have	drive	test
type	search	ask	build

State of being means "existing." Here are some being verbs.

be (am, is, are, was, were)	become	appear
seem	remain	continue
feel (as in emotion)		

How do you identify the verb in a sentence?

1   Read the sentence.

2   Identify the action or state of being. Ask: What is happening? If there is no action, look for the verb of being.

EXAMPLE

Underline the verb in this sentence.

Shawna sterilized the instruments.

1   Read the sentence.

2   What happened? sterilized—that is the verb.

Shawna <u>sterilized</u> the instruments.

EXAMPLE

Underline the verb in this sentence.

The salary is $8.30 an hour.

1   Read the sentence.

2   What is happening? Nothing. Look for the verb of being—is—salary is.

The salary <u>is</u> $8.30 an hour.

EXAMPLE

Write a verb for the sentence. More than one verb will be correct.

Erica _____ a word-processing manual.

1 Read the sentence.

2 Think of what the action could be between *Erica* and the *word processing manual*: dropped? used? tore? bought? saw? read? wrote? They are all good choices because they describe an action.

Erica __bought__ a word-processing manual.

PRACTICE

Underline the verb. If the verb is an action verb, write an A over it. If it is a state-of-being verb, write a B over it. The first one is done for you.

        A
1. Terry <u>works</u> for Dr. Reilly four days a week.

2. Brian's computer needs repair.

3. Mrs. Murdock hired an assistant.

4. John asked for a raise.

5. Debbie wrote the payroll program.

6. Andy answered the phone for me.

7. Jane became a secretary for the city.

8. Tim is a new member of the union.

9. Alex drew a diagram for a new circuit.

10. Erin was head of her own business.

Underline the verb that makes the most sense. The first one is done for you.

11. The computer (drove, <u>searched</u>) for the file.

12. (Send, Paint) the report to me as soon as you can.

13. Shavonne (takes, like) her break at 2 o'clock.

14. Kevin (shipped, turned) that order last week.

15. The service fee (has, is) $15.

16. Ladonna (found, made) an interview appointment today.

17. My father (refused, asked) another job transfer.

18. We (involved, discussed) the new health benefits.

19. Sean (was, will) the record holder for new sales.

20. Tracey (talked, referred) her patient to another agency.

L E S S O N   1 . 8

Verb Tenses

Objective   To form and use the correct tense of a verb.

The tense of a verb can express action in the present (today), the past (yesterday), or the future (tomorrow).

Present	Past	Future
He types quickly.	He typed that last week.	He will type it next Monday.

The spelling of the verb form usually changes with the tense. *Regular verbs* form the past tense by adding *-d* or *-ed* to the base verb. The future tense is formed by putting *will* in front of the base verb. *Shall* can also be used to form the future tense. *Shall* is used only if the subject is ''I'' or ''we''—I shall type, we shall type.

Regular verbs form the past tense by adding *-d* or *-ed* to the base verb.

| change | changed | | reserve | reserved |
| call | called | | assist | assisted |

EXAMPLE

Here are the tenses of some regular verbs.

Present	Past	Future
repair	repaired	will repair
test	tested	will test

Present	Past	Future
investigate	investigated	will investigate
prepare	prepared	will prepare
program	programmed	will program

PRACTICE

Fill in the blanks with the correct form of the verb. The first one is done for you.

Present	Past	Future
1. reserve	reserved	will reserve
2. _____	filled	_____
3. add	_____	_____
4. _____	_____	will order
5. attend	_____	_____
6. _____	managed	_____
7. _____	_____	will weld
8. check	_____	_____
9. _____	_____	will maintain
10. process	_____	_____
11. _____	examined	_____
12. _____	drafted	_____
13. _____	_____	will clean
14. file	_____	_____
15. mail	_____	_____
16. _____	counted	_____
17. _____	_____	will serve
18. _____	cooked	_____
19. receive	_____	_____
20. _____	talked	_____

Other Verb Forms

Objective   To recognize auxiliary verbs and to give the four principal parts of a verb.

The four principal parts of any verb are the present, present participle, past, and past participle.

The participles are formed by using an *auxiliary,* or *helping verb,* with the root verb. The auxiliary verbs are:

am	have	be	can	do	will
is	has	being	could	does	shall
are	had	been	would	did	may
was			should		might
were					must

The present participle is formed by using *am, is,* or *are* with the *-ing* form of the verb. Most verbs just add *-ing* to the root verb.

EXAMPLE

Present	Present Participle	
add	(am, is, are)	adding
stand	(am, is, are)	standing
cook	(am, is, are)	cooking
ring	(am, is, are)	ringing
order	(am, is, are)	ordering

If the verb ends in a single vowel followed by a single consonant (except *x* and *y*), double the consonant before adding *-ing.*

EXAMPLE

Present	Present Participle	
drop	(am, is, are)	dropping (Double the p.)
set	(am, is, are)	setting (Double the t.)

Present	Present Participle
skim	(am, is, are) skimming (Double the m.)
put	(am, is, are) putting (Double the t.)
jab	(am, is, are) jabbing (Double the b.)

But:

buy	(am, is, are) buying
fix	(am, is, are) fixing

If the verb ends in *-e*, drop the *-e* before adding *-ing*.

EXAMPLE

Present	Present Participle
sue	suing
write	writing
compute	computing
nurse	nursing

But:

lie	lying
die	dying

The past participle is formed by using *have, has,* or *had* with the past tense.

EXAMPLE

Past	Past Participle
entered	(have, has, had) entered
announced	(have, has, had) announced
helped	(have, has, had) helped
filled	(have, has, had) filled

As with the present participle, a single consonant that follows a single vowel is doubled when the *-ed* is added.

EXAMPLE

Past	Past Participle	
rubbed	(have, has, had)	rubbed
fitted	(have, has, had)	fitted

PRACTICE

Write the four principal parts of each verb. The first one is done for you.

Present	Present Participle (am, is, are)	Past	Past Participle (have, has, had)
1. prescribe	prescribing	prescribed	prescribed
2. remove			
3. analyze			
4. purchase			
5. practice			
6. listen			
7. respond			
8. learn			
9. decay			
10. establish			
11. discover			
12. type			
13. enter			
14. call			
15. prepare			

	Present	Present Participle (am, is, are)	Past	Past Participle (have, has, had)
16. clean	_____	_____	_____
17. store	_____	_____	_____
18. work	_____	_____	_____
19. complete	_____	_____	_____
20. estimate	_____	_____	_____

LESSON 1.10

Perfect Tenses

Objective   To use the correct forms of the perfect tenses.

The perfect tenses are present perfect, past perfect, and future perfect. They are formed by using *have, has, had,* or *will have* with the past participle.

	Present Perfect	Past Perfect	Future Perfect
Tense	Action that started in the past and is still happening.	Action that happened in the past before something else in the past.	Action that will happen in the future before something else happens.
Form	Use *have* with the past participle, except in the third person singular, when you use *has*.	Use *had* with the past participle.	Use *will have* with the past participle.
Example	We *have worked* together for three years. He *has worked* here for one year.	We *had worked* on the project for two years before you came.	We *will have worked* on it for four years before it is finished.

PRACTICE

Complete the following. The first one is done for you.

Present	Present Perfect	Past Perfect	Future Perfect
1. purchase	has or have purchased	had purchased	will have purchased
2. ask	_____	_____	_____
3. watch	_____	_____	_____
4. record	_____	_____	_____
5. employ	_____	_____	_____
6. use	_____	_____	_____
7. audit	_____	_____	_____
8. increase	_____	_____	_____
9. express	_____	_____	_____
10. defend	_____	_____	_____

Complete each sentence with the required tense. The first one is done for you.

11. Leon (future perfect of bake) will have baked 100 pies for his catering business before Thanksgiving.

12. Kendra (past perfect of form) _____ an opinion of her before she even met her.

13. You (present perfect of earn) _____ more money than I ever will.

14. My legal assistant (future perfect of research)_____ it before our appointment.

15. He (past perfect of <u>repair</u>) _____ his computer just before he sold it.

16. Sherry already (past perfect of <u>type</u>) _____ the letter when her boss decided to make a change.

17. Ms. Adams (present perfect of <u>request</u>) _____ the same flight as she had the last time.

18. I (present perfect of <u>order</u>) _____ new chairs for my new office.

19. Allen's idea (future perfect of <u>save</u>) _____ the company thousands of dollars by the end of the year.

20. Mr. Silvers (present perfect of <u>promote</u>) _____ me to assistant head teller.

Progressive Tenses

Objective   To form and use the progressive tenses.

The progressive tenses express action that is in progress—action that is going on or continuing. They are formed by using auxiliary verbs with the present participle.

	Present Progressive	Past Progressive	Future Progressive
Tense	Action that IS in progress now.	Action that WAS in progress then.	Action that WILL BE in progress in the future.
Form	*1st Person* I *am* thinking. We *are* thinking. *2nd Person* You *are* thinking. *3rd Person* He *is* thinking. They *are* thinking.	*1st Person* I *was* thinking. We *were* thinking. *2nd Person* You *were* thinking. *3rd Person* He *was* thinking. They *were* thinking.	*1st Person* I *will be* thinking. We *will be* thinking. *2nd Person* You *will be* thinking. *3rd Person* He *will be* thinking. They *will be* thinking.
Example	We *are thinking* about a new secretary right now.	You *were thinking* about a new secretary when I talked to you last week.	They *will be thinking* about a new secretary as soon as the position is definite.

	Present Perfect Progressive	Past Perfect Progressive	Future Perfect Progressive
Tense	Action that began in the past and IS STILL in progress.	Action that WAS in progress in the past before something else in the past.	Action that WILL BE in progress in the future before something else happens.
Form	Use *have been* with the present participle, except in the third person singular, when you use *has been*.	Use *had been* with the present participle.	Use *will have been* with the present participle.
Example	I *have been thinking* all day. He *has been thinking* all day, too.	She *had been thinking* about it for a long time.	They *will have been thinking* about this for two weeks by the time they make a decision.

PRACTICE

Write the required tense. Use third person singular (he, she, it) for each. The first one is done for you.

1. interpret (past progressive)   he was interpreting
2. occupy (present progressive)   she has occuping
3. replace (future perfect progressive)   he will be replacing
4. delay (present perfect progressive)   _____
5. devise (past perfect progressive)   _____
6. monitor (future progressive)   _____
7. produce (present progressive)   _____
8. examine (past perfect progressive   _____
9. manage (future progressive)   _____
10. order (past progressive)   _____

Each sentence uses the progressive tense of the verb. Write the correct helping verb or verbs for the required form. The first one is done for you.

11. Present progressive—We _____are_____ considering two different models of printers.

12. Future perfect progressive—They _____ looking for new office space for two years by the end of May.

13. Past progressive—You _____ checking on my reservations when I interrupted you.

14. Present perfect progressive—He _____ working on that estimate for a week.

15. Future progressive—I _____ scanning this electronics catalog while you take your break.

16. Past perfect progressive—He _____ collecting data for the new project for over a year when it was canceled.

17. Future progressive—She _____ recording your interest income while you endorse that check.

18. Present progressive—You _____ saving yourself a lot of money by buying used office furniture.

19. Present perfect progressive—We _____ following your advice faithfully.

20. Past progressive—They _____ planning to announce the new merger at the sales conference.

Irregular Verbs

Objective   To learn the principal parts of irregular verbs and to form the various tenses.

Irregular verbs form the past tense in some way other than adding *-d* or *-ed* to the base verb as regular verbs do.

bring	brought	hold	held
lose	lost	leave	left

Verbs that do not follow the usual pattern of adding *-ed* to form the past and past participle are called **irregular verbs.**

Most irregular verbs are used often, and you should study the following lists until all the verb forms are familiar to you.

A. The present, past, and past participle are the same word.

Present	Present Participle	Past	Past Participle
beat	beating	beat	beat (or beaten)
bet	betting	bet	bet
bid	bidding	bid	bid
burst	bursting	burst	burst
cost	costing	cost	cost
fit	fitting	fit	fit
hit	hitting	hit	hit
hurt	hurting	hurt	hurt
put	putting	put	put
read	reading	read	read (pronounced ''red'')
set	setting	set	set
shut	shutting	shut	shut
sleep	sleeping	slept	slept
spread	spreading	spread	spread

B. The past and past participle are the same.

Present	Present Participle	Past	Past Participle
bend	bending	bent	bent
bring	bringing	brought	brought
buy	buying	bought	bought
catch	catching	caught	caught
cling	clinging	clung	clung
creep	creeping	crept	crept
deal	dealing	dealt	dealt
fight	fighting	fought	fought
find	finding	found	found
fling	flinging	flung	flung
have	having	had	had
hear	hearing	heard	heard
hold	holding	held	held
keep	keeping	kept	kept

Present	Present Participle	Past	Past Participle
lay	laying	laid	laid
lead	leading	led	led
leave	leaving	left	left
lend	lending	lent	lent
lose	losing	lost	lost
meet	meeting	met	met
pay	paying	paid	paid
seek	seeking	sought	sought
*shine	shining	shone	shone
sit	sitting	sat	sat
sting	stinging	stung	stung
swing	swinging	swung	swung
teach	teaching	taught	taught
think	thinking	thought	thought
strike	striking	struck	struck
tell	telling	told	told
stand	standing	stood	stood
say	saying	said	said
wring	wringing	wrung	wrung

*Meaning ''to give off light.'' When *shine* means ''to polish,'' it is a regular verb—the past and past particple are *shined*.

C. The vowel in the present changes to -*a* for the past and to -*u* for the past participle.

Present	Present Participle	Past	Past Participle
begin	beginning	began	begun
drink	drinking	drank	drunk
ring	ringing	rang	rung
run	running	ran	run
sing	singing	sang	sung
sink	sinking	sank	sunk
spring	springing	sprang	sprung

Present	Present Participle	Past	Past Participle
swim	swimming	swam	swum
shrink	shrinking	shrank	shrunk

D. The past participle is formed by adding *-n, -en,* or *-ne* to the present or *-n* or *-en* to the past. The form of the present or past may vary somewhat.

Present	Present Participle	Past	Past Participle
be (am, is, are)	being	was	been
bite	biting	bit	bitten
blow	blowing	blew	blown
break	breaking	broke	broken
choose	choosing	chose	chosen
do	doing	did	done
draw	drawing	drew	drawn
drive	driving	drove	driven
eat	eating	ate	eaten
fly	flying	flew	flown
fall	falling	fell	fallen
forget	forgetting	forgot	forgotten
freeze	freezing	froze	frozen
get	getting	got	gotten
give	giving	gave	given
go	going	went	gone
grow	growing	grew	grown
hide	hiding	hid	hidden
know	knowing	knew	known
lie	lying	lay	lain
ride	riding	rode	ridden
rise	rising	rose	risen
see	seeing	saw	seen
shake	shaking	shook	shaken
speak	speaking	spoke	spoken
steal	stealing	stole	stolen
swear	swearing	swore	sworn
take	taking	took	taken

Present	Present Participle	Past	Past Participle
tear	tearing	tore	torn
throw	throwing	threw	thrown
wake	waking	woke	woken
wear	wearing	wore	worn
write	writing	wrote	written

EXAMPLE

Complete: (present perfect of *go*) You _____ .

1 Find *go* in the list.

2 The past participle is *gone*.
To form the present perfect, put *have* in front of the past participle.

3 Fill in the blank. You ___have gone___ .

PRACTICE

Complete. The first one is done for you. (Look back at Lessons 1.8 and 1.10 if you need help forming the tenses.)

1. (past of *run*) He ___ran_____ .
2. (future perfect of *grow*) We _____ .
3. (past perfect of *take*) You _____ .
4. (present perfect of *buy*) They _____ .
5. (past of *begin*) I _____ .
6. (present perfect of *draw*) She _____ .
7. (past perfect of *write*) You _____ .
8. (future perfect of *read*) I _____ .
9. (past of *lend*) They _____ .
10. (past perfect of *pay*) We _____ .
11. (past of *meet*) He _____ .
12. (present perfect of *bid*) They _____ .
13. (future perfect of *have*) We _____ .
14. (past of *speak*) You _____ .

15. (present perfect of *choose*) I _____ .

16. (future perfect of *cost*) It _____ .

17. (past of *know*) They _____ .

18. (future perfect of *teach*) She _____ .

19. (past perfect of *forget*) I _____ .

20. (present perfect of *deal*) You _____ .

LESSON 1.13

Adjectives

Objective   To recognize the different kinds of adjectives.

An **adjective** is a word that modifies a noun or pronoun. *Modifies* means "describes" or "changes."

Adjectives make writing more interesting and more exact.

- If you just say that you typed letters, you have not given the listener very much information.

- If you say you typed *30* letters, the listener has an idea of how much typing you did.

- If you say you typed *30 long* letters, the listener has an even better idea of how much typing you did.

Most adjectives are called *descriptive* adjectives.

six days	*blue* napkins	*first* job
small staff	*good* X ray	*clear* directions

There are special kinds of adjectives.

A. *Proper* adjectives are made from proper nouns, often by adding *-n, -ese,* or *-ian* to the noun.

EXAMPLE

If you were born in America, you are *American*.

If your computer was made in Japan, it is *Japanese*.

If the parent company of the firm for which you work is head-quartered in Italy, you work for an *Italian* firm.

B. *Possessive* adjectives can be possessive pronouns that modify nouns or they can be the possessive form of a noun.

EXAMPLE

my résumé   *your* contract
Mr. Young's office   *California's* business

C. The words *a, an,* and *the* are special adjectives called *articles.*

A and *an* are *indefinite articles.*

The is the *definite article.*

EXAMPLE

A is used before words that begin with a consonant or a long-sounding *u* *(a unit).*

An is used before words that begin with *a, e, i, o,* or a short-sounding *u,* or words that sound like they begin with a vowel *(an hour).*

D. The demonstrative pronouns, *this, that, these,* and *those,* can be used as *demonstrative adjectives.* They point something out.

EXAMPLE

this job   *those* results

E. If nouns and verbs modify nouns, they are used as adjectives. They do not have a special name.

EXAMPLE

cafeteria meal—noun used as adjective

scheduled meeting—verb used as adjective

F. *Compound* adjectives are formed when two or more words act like one word. They are often hyphenated.

state-of-the-art equipment

first-rate job

two-page report

But:

human services office

high school diploma

A good dictionary can usually show you which compounds are hyphenated if you are confused about them.

PRACTICE

Underline the adjectives. The first one is done for you.

1. The summer merchandise is on sale to make room for the new fall clothes.
2. You are the first appointment of the day.
3. Have your recent résumé printed on good white paper.
4. The dental assistant did a careful and complete job on cleaning her teeth.
5. A welder wears safety goggles.
6. A computer-repair person uses many special tools.
7. The auto-body shop will be able to remove the terrible dent from the front fender.
8. She made her reservations for the 6 o'clock flight.
9. An efficient and caring nurse's aide is a valuable employee in any hospital.
10. The copies from that old machine need to be done over.

Name the kind of adjective. The first one is done for you.

11. *French* firm   _____proper_____
12. *the* manager   _____
13. *computer* paper   _____
14. *necessary* test   _____
15. *first-rate* service   _____
16. *that* laboratory   _____
17. *favorite* restaurant   _____
18. *new* administration   _____
19. *teller's* salary   _____
20. *six-digit* number   _____

LESSON 1.14

Comparison of Adjectives

Objective   To form and correctly use the comparative and superlative degrees of an adjective.

Adjectives have three degrees of comparison:

1. Positive degree: This is the "regular" pronoun; nothing is being compared.

   This is an *easy* job.

2. Comparative degree: One thing is being compared with another. The comparative ends in *-er*.

   This is an *easier* job than my last one.

3. Superlative degree: Three or more things are compared. The superlative ends in *-est*.

   This is the *easiest* job I ever had.

Note: The *y* in *easy* changed to *i* before the *-er* and *-est* were added to *easy*.

The spelling changes that are necessary when comparing adjectives follow the same rules as for forming various verb forms.

1. The final consonant is doubled if a short-sounding vowel is followed by a single consonant.

hot	hotter	hottest
red	redder	reddest

But: quick   quicker   quickest

2. If the last letter in a word is *-e*, it is dropped before adding *-er* or *-est*.

   fine   finer   finest

3. If the last letter in a word is *y*, it is changed to *i* before adding *-er* or *-est*.

   heavy   heavier   heaviest

Some adjectives have irregular comparative and superlative forms.

Positive	Comparative	Superlative
well (health) good	better	best
bad ill	worse	worst
much many	more	most
little (in amount)	less	least
far	farther	farthest

Words of *three or more syllables* form the comparative by putting *more* or *less* in front of the word. They form the superlative by putting *most* or *least* in front of the word.

| expensive | more expensive | most expensive |
| | less expensive | least expensive |

(*Expensiver* or *expensivest* would be awkward to pronounce.)

More/less and *most/least* are also used with some two-syllable words that sound awkward with *-er* and *-est* and with two-syllable words that end in *-ful, -less, -some,* or *-r.*

frequent	more frequent	most frequent
	less frequent	least frequent
careful	more careful	most careful
	less careful	least careful
eager	more/less eager	most/least eager
wholesome	more/less wholesome	most/least wholesome
tactless	more/less tactless	most/least tactless

Never use the double comparison. Do not write:

~~more~~ better   ~~most~~ earliest

Some adjectives cannot sensibly be compared:

If something is *perfect,* something else cannot be more perfect.

If something is *correct,* something else cannot be more or less correct.

If something is *empty,* other things cannot be the most empty.

Adjectives of this type express an absolute condition that cannot be compared. Other examples are *alive, dead, right, wrong,* and *straight.*

PRACTICE

Form the comparative and superlative. The first one is done for you.

Positive	Comparative	Superlative
1. fast	faster	fastest
2. skillful	_____	_____
3. strong	_____	_____
4. healthful	_____	_____

Positive	Comparative	Superlative
5. late	_____	_____
6. valuable	_____	_____
7. intelligent	_____	_____
8. sour	_____	_____
9. careless	_____	_____
10. self-confident	_____	_____
11. good	_____	_____
12. dangerous	_____	_____
13. boring	_____	_____
14. tasty	_____	_____
15. talented	_____	_____
16. popular	_____	_____
17. thin	_____	_____
18. unhealthy	_____	_____
19. sloppy	_____	_____
20. efficient	_____	_____

LESSON 1.15

Adverbs

Objective   To recognize and use adverbs.

An **adverb** is a word that modifies a verb, an adjective, or another adverb.

EXAMPLE

She followed the directions exactly.

Verb	Adverb
followed	exactly

That disk is almost full.

Adverb	Adjective
almost	full

He caught on to the new program very quickly.

Adverb	Adverb
very	quickly

Adverbs make writing more interesting, just as adjectives do. Many adverbs end in *-ly*, but not all do. Not all *-ly* words are adverbs.

frequently is an adverb, but *early* is not.

often is an adverb, but does not end in *ly*.

Adverbs answer the questions *how? when? where? how often?* and *to what extent?*

EXAMPLE

- He handled the computer carefully.
  Handled *how*? carefully.
- She typed the letter yesterday.
  Typed *when*? yesterday.
- He likes to work outside.
  Work *where*? outside.
- They are always looking for new salespeople.
  Looking *when*? always.
- I was very happy with your report.
  Happy *to what extent*? very.

Sometimes adverbs are used incorrectly.

Drive slowly

means ''slowly go through the action of driving''—but the car could be going 80 miles per hour. What is usually wanted is:

Drive slow

which means ''Drive so that the car goes slow.''
Some adverbs can be compared like adjectives.

fast	faster	fastest
quickly	more quickly	most quickly

Be sure to use *well,* not *good,* when an adverb is required. *Good* is an adjective.

> He uses the program well. (adverb—*well*)

> He is a good programmer. (adjective—*good*)

Irregular Comparisons		
well	better	best
bad	worse	worst
much	more	most
little	less	least
far	farther	farthest

PRACTICE

Underline the adverbs in each sentence. The first one is done for you.

1. The <u>newly</u> furnished office will be a <u>more</u> pleasant place in which to work.

2. This organization plan has things running more smoothly than before.

3. The workers complained loudly about the most recent pay cuts.

4. An emergency medical technician is trained to work quickly and carefully.

5. The boss spoke well of your plans.

6. Anyone in food service learns that it is important to clean vegetables thoroughly.

7. Jenny works more efficiently than her partner.

8. The salespeople were told to aggressively market these very expensive products.

9. That badly warped floor can only be fixed by a skilled craftsperson.

10. The printing press stopped suddenly when the power went off.

Underline each adverb, and draw an arrow to the word it modifies. The first one is done for you.

11. Max <u>proudly</u> told his friends about his job.

12. Very skilled programmers will work on that project.

13. He gently put the new computer chip in place.

14. He often calls the IRS with tax problems.

15. Michelle steadily improved her skills as a word processor.

16. Andy did not mind the slow work of filing the legal papers.

17. Lisa is good on the phone because she speaks distinctly and not too fast.

18. That order should have gone out promptly on the first of the month.

19. You should always arrive early for an interview.

20. The patient would speak only to me.

Prepositions and Prepositional Phrases

Objective   To identify prepositions, prepositional phrases, and the object of a preposition.

A **preposition** is a word (or words) that shows the relationship between a noun or pronouns and another word in a sentence.

A **prepositional phrase** is a preposition with its object (a noun or pronoun) and any words between the preposition and its object.

Suppose you have a chair and a desk. The chair can be related to the desk in many ways. It can be *on* the desk, *beside* the desk, *under* the desk, *behind* the desk, *near* the desk, *next to* the desk, and so on.

On, beside, under, behind, near, and *next to* are prepositions. The following is a list of the prepositions used most often.

aboard	because of	down	like	through
about	before	during	near	throughout
above	behind	except	next to	till
according to	below	for	of	to
across	beneath	from	off	toward
after	beside	in	on	under
against	besides	in back of	onto	underneath
along	between	in front of	out	until
alongside	beyond	in place of	out of	up
alongside of	but	in spite of	outside	upon
among	by	instead	over	with
around	concerning	instead of	past	within
at	despite	into	since	without

Read the list a few times until the prepositions are familiar. To identify a prepositional phrase:

1 Read a sentence until you come to a preposition.

2 Ask the question "what?" after the preposition. That locates the object of the preposition and the end of the phrase.

3 If the sentence is longer, continue reading to see if there is another prepositional phrase.

EXAMPLE

My new office is *on the second floor*.

1 *on* is the preposition.

2 *on* what? on floor—*floor* is the object of the preposition, so the phrase is *on the second floor*.

3 That is the end of the sentence.

EXAMPLE

Jesse's office is *in that building across the street*.

1 *in* is the preposition.

2 *in* what? in building—*building* is the object of the preposition, so the prepositional phrase is *in that building*.

3 The sentence continues, so continue reading.

1 *across* is the preposition.

2 *across* what? across street—*street* is the object of the preposition, so the phrase is *across the street*.

3 That is the end of the sentence.

A prepositional phrase can be classified as an adjective phrase or an adverb phrase.

The phrase is an *adjective phrase* if it modifies a noun.

The phrase is an *adverb phrase* if it modifies a verb, adjective, or another adverb.

EXAMPLE

Look at this sentence again:

> Jesse's office is *in that building across the street.*
>
> in the building is an *adverb* phrase, modifies *is,* tells *where.*
>
> *across the street* is an *adjective phrase,* modifies *building,* tells *which* building.

PRACTICE

Underline the prepositions in each sentence. The first one is done for you.

1. The mail room is <u>at</u> the end <u>of</u> the hall.
2. My interview is at 2 o'clock on Thursday.
3. Court is in session from 9:30 A.M. until 1:00 P.M.
4. The coffee machine is on the counter next to the microwave.
5. Throughout history, doctors have had aides working beside them.
6. The copy machine is out of order and was sent for repair.
7. She went on a tour of the electronics department instead of the drafting department.
8. He is taking a job as a dental assistant in a small town outside of Philadelphia.
9. Despite her natural cooking skills, Kenyatta needs formal training in food service.
10. The report concerning the new project will arrive by messenger this afternoon.

Underline the prepositional phrase, and draw a second line under the object of the preposition. The first one is done for you.

11. <u>Between <u>you</u> and <u>me</u></u>, this is the best job I have had <u>since <u>graduation</u></u>.
12. I placed your copy of the letter under your paperweight.
13. The computer repair store had its rates posted on the wall above the telephone.
14. The dental assistant fastened a napkin around the patient's neck.
15. The bank is open until 5:00 P.M. every day of the week.
16. The sales manager outlined the goals toward which we should work.
17. The head of the union was against longer workdays.
18. The blood bank always experiences shortages during the holidays.

19. Scott arranged the appetizers for the banquet, placing the crackers alongside the cheese and behind the vegetables.

20. The body shop replaced the bumper that had fallen off my car after the accident.

L E S S O N   1 . 1 7

Preposition Problems

Objective   To be aware of possible errors in the use of prepositions and to use prepositions correctly.

1. *to:* If *to* is followed by a verb, it indicates the *infinitive form* of the verb, not a prepositional phrase.

EXAMPLE

Computer programmers often like *to work* alone.

work is a verb, an action word, so *to work* is an infinitive.

They promised *to ship* the order to you by Friday.

ship is a verb, so *to ship* is an infinitive.

Note: *you* is a pronoun, so *to you* is a prepositional phrase.

2. *between* and *among:* Use *between* for two people or things. Use *among* for more than two people or things.

EXAMPLE

The counter is a divider *between* the *sales area* and the *repair area*. (between two things)

New accounts are distributed evenly *among* the *four salespeople*. (among four people)

3. *in* and *into:* Use *in* when something is contained in another. Use *into* to show motion from one place to another.

EXAMPLE

The computer is *in* my office.

I brought the laptop computer *into* the office today.

4. *off* and *from:* Use *off* (never *off of*) only when something is actually taken off something.

EXAMPLE

I took the telephone book *off* the shelf.

I borrowed a telephone book *from* him.

Note: *from* (not *than*) is always used after the word *different*.

EXAMPLE

Computers are very *different from* what they were in the 1950s.

5. *beside* and *besides:* Use *beside* when something is *next to* something else. Use *besides* when something is *in addition to* something else.

EXAMPLE

I placed my briefcase *beside* (next to) my desk.

I carried a handbag *besides* (in addition to) my briefcase.

6. *speak to* and *speak with:* Use *speak to* when someone is telling something to someone. Use *speak with* when something is being discussed.

EXAMPLE

I would like to *speak to* you about your schedule. (*tell* you about your schedule)

I would like to *speak with* you about our vacation policies. (*discuss* the vacation policies)

7. *like* and *as:* Use *like* when you need a preposition. *As* is a conjunction, used with a clause, which is taught in Lesson 2.7.

EXAMPLE

That letter does not look *like* a copy.

I opened the door *as* the phone was ringing.

8. Be sure to put prepositions with their objects. A preposition should not be alone at the end of a sentence.

EXAMPLE

This is the office *in which* you will work.

NOT This is the office you will work *in*.

I will send a copy to the salesperson *to whom* you referred.
NOT I will send a copy to the salesperson you referred *to*.

From whom did you get that information?
NOT Who did you get that information *from*?

A pronoun as the object of a preposition will be treated in Lesson 2.5.

PRACTICE

Underline the correct word or words. The first one is done for you.

1. The profits will be divided (between, <u>among</u>) all the employees.
2. I got a mop (off, from) the janitor.
3. This is different (from, than) what I expected.
4. (Beside, Besides) other responsibilities, an office assistant will schedule appointments.
5. I will (speak with, speak to) the staff about the extra holiday.
6. Take those pictures (off, from) the wall.
7. When Patrice arrived at the meeting, the only empty seat was (between, among) the president and me.
8. The withdrawal slips are right (beside, besides) the deposit slips.
9. All the paintings had to be moved (in, into) the storeroom so the walls could be repainted.
10. After work, I would like to (speak with, speak to) you about planning the retirement party.

Each sentence contains an error. Rewrite it correctly. The first one is done for you.

11. This is the program she was talking about.

    This is the program about which she was talking.

    _____

12. When Paul had his car repainted, the color was very different than what he expected.

    _____

    _____

13. Beside plane reservations, the travel agent also made hotel reservations.

    _____

    _____

14. When the computer crashed, we had to borrow a backup disk off my brother.

_____

_____

15. The presentation at the dinner went very well because the slide projector was right besides the speakers' table.

_____

_____

16. After Marisol received her award, she stepped off of the platform.

_____

_____

17. Speak to your supervisor about any schedule changes you might like.

_____

_____

18. Who did you send invitations to?

_____

_____

19. The catering director left to get a menu off the waitress.

_____

_____

20. Since Janelle was the newest employee, she could only choose among two vacation weeks.

_____

_____

LESSON 1.18

Conjunctions

Objective   To recognize conjunctions and their proper use.

A **conjunction** is a word (or words) that joins other words or groups of words.

Two kinds of conjunctions are *coordinating conjunctions* and *correlative conjunctions*.

1. Coordinating conjunctions join similar words or groups of words in a sentence.

   and   or   nor   for   so   but   yet

   EXAMPLE

   Shawanda **and** *I* work together.

   Steve will *buy* **or** *lease* a delivery van.

   Michael likes business, **but** *his sister prefers nursing.*

   Hang your uniform *on a hanger* **or** *on a hook.*

2. Correlative conjunctions are used in pairs to join similar words or groups of words in a sentence.

both . . . and	either . . . or	neither . . . nor
just as . . . so	not only . . . but (also)	whether . . . or

   EXAMPLE

   The new position was offered to **both** *Diana* **and** *her.*

   You can take your pay **either** *in cash* **or** *as a check.*

   Not only *am I being transferred,* **but** *I am being promoted.*

   PRACTICE

Underline the conjunction and identify it as coordinating or correlative. The first one is done for you.

1. The purchasing office will accept <u>either</u> your bid <u>or</u> mine.   _____correlative_____

2. The chairman was not sure if he would call the meeting for Wednesday or Friday.   _____

3. A temporary secretary has been hired so Alice can attend the convention.   _____

4. Tom acts as both teller and manager at this bank.   _____

5. Patrice takes not only a train but also a bus to commute to work.   _____

6. Just as Paul always wanted to be an electrician, so did his twin brother always want to be a carpenter.   _____

7. The special in the cafeteria today is spaghetti and meatballs.   _____

8. Neither plastic nor aluminum is strong enough for the part I need.   _____

9. Whether the store stays open or closes will depend on this quarter's earnings.   _____

10. She thought of going into hotel management but chose a food-service career instead.   _____

Underline the words or groups of words that are joined by a conjunction. The first one is done for you.

11. The dental assistant tells all her patients how important <u>brushing</u> and <u>flossing</u> are.

12. Marco is being transferred to either the Boston or the Washington, D.C., office.

13. Frank thought of being an auto mechanic, but he became a welder instead.

14. Whether the office opens today or tomorrow depends on when the repairs are finished.

15. Neither Anne nor her assistant could get the computer to boot up.

16. Mr. Murphy needed to be in Chicago that day, so he decided to fly.

17. Not only banks but credit unions must have adequate insurance to cover their deposits.

18. Just as hundreds of our students have gotten good jobs after graduation, so can you.

19. That computer printer can print in color or in black and white.

20. Ayeesha has trained to be both a legal and a medical secretary.

LESSON 1.19

Interjections

Objective   To recognize and use interjections.

An **interjection** is a word (or group of words) that expresses strong or sudden feeling, like anger, surprise, or joy.

An interjection has no relation to the rest of the sentence and so is separated from the sentence by an exclamation point to show strong feeling or a comma to show milder feeling.

You probably use interjections every day in speaking.

EXAMPLE

Oh, no! I forgot my lunch.

Great! The new disk drive was delivered.

Well, I will think about your suggestion.

Interjections could be called the *human* element of speech or writing, but they are not usually used in formal or business writing.

Common Interjections

ah	gosh	hush	oh, my	ugh
aha	hey	my goodness	oh, no	well
bravo	hooray	oh	oops	whoopee
gee	hurrah	oh, dear	ouch	wow

Other kinds of words can be used as interjections.

Noun: Nonsense! Congratulations!

Adjective: Good! Sorry! Not!

Verb: Help!

PRACTICE

Underline the interjection. The first one is done for you.

1. Quiet! We cannot hear the instructions.
2. Help! The paper has jammed in the printer.
3. Oh, I think you can learn to use a word processor.
4. Well, you know which job is best for you.
5. Hey! I have another letter for you.
6. We are getting a raise. Hooray!
7. Well! That technician knows how to do a painless blood test.
8. Congratulations! You deserved the promotion.
9. Wow! This refrigerator must be 30 years old.
10. Sorry, we have no vacancy.

Write an interjection that could fit the sentence. The first one is done for you.

11. _____Great!_____ You found the manual.

12. _____, you can try your method and see if it works.

13. _____ The buffet looks very appetizing.

14. _____ I got a paper cut from that envelope.

15. _____ The copy machine needs toner.

Basic Sentence Structure

A Sentence, Subject and Predicate

Objective   To recognize a sentence as a complete thought and to identify the subject and predicate.

A **sentence** is a word or group of words that expresses a complete thought. It begins with a capital letter and ends with an end punctuation mark.

A sentence can have any number of words.

EXAMPLE

a. The desk is new.
b. Go away!
c. Work.
d. Help me, please.
e. Are you the boss?
f. She can type.
g. Wow! Can she type!
h. The supply room is the first door on the left.
i. David should talk to the receptionist.
j. Working hard and enjoying my work are most important to me right now.

All of the above examples are sentences.

1 Each expresses a complete thought.

2 Each begins with a capital letter.

3 Each ends with a punctuation mark.

To express a complete thought, a sentence must have two parts: a *subject* and a *predicate*.

> A **subject** can be a noun or a pronoun. The subject names a person, place, or thing about which something is being told.
>
> The **predicate** is a verb, which may or may not have auxiliary verbs. The predicate tells what the subject does or is.

Note that *subject* and *predicate* are sentence parts. *Noun, pronoun,* and *verb* are parts of speech.

Look again at example (a): desk is the subject, is is the predicate.

The desk is new.

In example (b): Go is the predicate. It does not look like the sentence has a subject, but it does. One person is telling another to go away. "Go away" is the same as "You go away." The subject You is understood.

(You) Go away!

In example (c): You is the subject understood.

Work means (You) Work.

Look at examples (d)–(i). To identify subject and predicate, find the verb first and identify the complete predicate. Then find the subject by asking *who* or *what* before the predicate. The subject is underlined once, the predicate twice.

d.   Help me, please. (Subject is you understood.)

e.   Are you the boss?

f.   She can type.

g.   Can she type!

h.   The supply room is the first door on the left.

i.   David should talk to the receptionist.

> A **compound subject** is two or more nouns or pronouns that are joined by a conjunction and that have the same predicate.

In example (j): <u>Working</u> and <u>enjoying</u> is a compound subject. The predicate is one verb, <u>are</u>.

j.   <u>Working</u> hard and <u>enjoying</u> my work <u>are</u> most important to me right now.

> A **compound predicate** is two or more verbs with the same subject.

Julie <u>works</u> and <u>goes</u> to school at night.
The paper <u>slipped</u> and <u>jammed</u> the copy machine.

The following do *not* express a complete thought. They are sentence *fragments* (or parts).

The laboratory
on my desk
walks and jogs to work
when the schedules are complete

Is it a sentence? Write Yes on the blank if it is. The first one is done for you.

1. Yasmeen would like to be a legal assistant.   _____Yes_____
2. Daniel handles security for the hotel.   _____
3. The newest laser-jet printer.   _____
4. Richard and his partner.   _____
5. Left for vacation yesterday.   _____
6. Send it now.   _____
7. Is Jerry getting a commission?   _____
8. As soon as I check your references.   _____
9. Follow my advice.   _____
10. In the back of the top file drawer.   _____

Underline the subject once and the predicate twice. The first one is done for you.

11. The <u>repairperson</u> <u>advised</u> the purchase of a new keyboard.

12. Many hotels now use card keys instead of metal room keys.

13. Mrs. Clarke bought a service contract for her refrigerator.

14. Robots can increase job safety by doing dangerous jobs.

15. Maria types all her letters on a word processor.

16. Jennifer's accountant called and advised her to buy a house.

17. He is studying to be a lab technician.

18. Michael and Luis received pay raises last week.

19. Only a professional should add coolant to a home air conditioner.

20. The New England states have many country inns.

Kinds of Sentences

Objective   To identify the four kinds of sentences.

You learned that a sentence expresses a complete thought and begins with a capital letter and ends with a punctuation mark. The examples in Lesson 2.1 showed three different end punctuation marks: .   ?   and   !

. is a period.

? is a question mark.

! is an exclamation point.

The four kinds of sentences are:

1. Declarative.
2. Interrogative.
3. Imperative.
4. Exclamatory.

1. A *declarative sentence* makes a statement or states a fact—it *declares* something. It ends with a period.

EXAMPLE

I have an associate's degree in electronics.
Steve will be the assistant manager when Andrea is promoted.

2. An *interrogative sentence* asks a direct question. It ends with a question mark. It often begins with an *interrogative pronoun: who, which, what, whom, whose. When, where, how,* and *why* are adverbs that may also begin interrogative sentences.

EXAMPLE

When will the report be finished?

Who is working on that project?

How many résumés did you send out?

Note that an *indirect question* states that a question was asked. It is a *declarative sentence.* The following show the interrogative sentences above changed to indirect questions

EXAMPLE

My supervisor asked when the report would be finished.

I wondered who was working on that project.

She wanted to know how many résumés you sent out.

3. An *imperative sentence* states a command or a request. It usually ends with a period, unless it is a very strong statement. The subject is usually *you* understood.

EXAMPLE

Fax it to me in the morning.

Please make an appointment with my secretary.

You must remember to change the access code every day.

Turn off that machine right now!

4. An *exclamatory sentence* expresses strong feeling or surprise. It ends with an exclamation point.

EXAMPLE

That's a great job!

What a terrific idea you had!

How smoothly you work together!

PRACTICE

Name the kind of sentence. The first one is done for you.

1. Who is the manager here?   _____interrogative_____

2. Rob became a programmer in two years.   _____

3. Please serve the second course.   _____

4. Will your raise put your income into a
   higher tax bracket?   _____

5. Was I surprised to get that job!   _____

6. Move the filing cabinet to the left.   _____

7. I knew you could figure it out!   _____

8. The new monitor will be delivered tomorrow.   _____

9. Always change the oil filter when you
   change the oil in your car.   _____

10. It will only take a few minutes to check
    your X rays.   _____

Copy the sentence so it begins and ends correctly. The first one is done for you.

11. robots can increase job safety by performing jobs that are dangerous for
    humans

    Robots can increase job safety by performing jobs that are dangerous for
    humans.

12. is a service contract a good buy

    _____

    _____

13. a salesperson usually gets a discount on any purchase where he or she
    works

    _____

    _____

14. what a lovely display that is

    _____

    _____

15. fill out the application and sign it

_____

_____

16. does your business use seasonal workers

_____

_____

17. how steadily you hold those instruments

_____

_____

18. all the words in three average novels can be put on one floppy disk

_____

_____

19. how cold should the inside of a good freezer be

_____

_____

20. please show me detailed drawings of your idea

_____

_____

LESSON 2.3

Direct Object, Indirect Object

Objective   To identify a direct object and an indirect object.

A **direct object** is a noun or pronoun that receives the action of the predicate.

To identify a direct object, ask ''whom'' or ''what'' after the predicate.

EXAMPLE

A draftsman makes detailed architectural drawings for use in construction.

1   The action of the sentence is *makes,* the predicate.

2 Who or what *makes?*
draftsman makes.
draftsman is the subject.

3 *draftsman makes* what?
draftsman makes *drawings*.
drawings is the direct object.

Note: *detailed* and *architectural* are adjectives that modify *drawings*, but they are not what the draftsman makes.

EXAMPLE

Evan is taking his secretary to lunch.

1 The action of the sentence is *is taking*, the predicate.

2 Who or what *is taking?*
Evan is taking.
Evan is the subject.

3 *Evan is taking* whom?
Evan is taking *secretary*.
secretary is the direct object.

An **indirect object** is a noun or pronoun *to* or *for* which the action of the predicate is done.

To identify an indirect object, ask: ''*to* or *for* whom or what'' after the predicate.

EXAMPLE

The sales representative sent Tyrone the samples.

1 The action of the sentence is *sent*, the predicate.

2 Who *sent?*
representative sent.
representative is the subject.

3 *representative sent* to whom?
representative sent to *Tyrone*.
Tyrone is the indirect object. The word *to* is understood in the sentence.

EXAMPLE

Carol bought the office a new microwave oven.

1 The action of the sentence is *bought*, the predicate.

2 Who *bought*?
Carol bought.
Carol is the subject.

3 *Carol bought* for what?
Carol bought for *office*.
office is the indirect object. The word *for* is understood in the sentence.

Pronouns as direct objects and indirect objects will be treated in Lesson 2.5.

PRACTICE

Underline the predicate with one line and the direct object with two lines. The first one is done for you.

1. A mechanic usually buys long-lasting tools.
2. Marcy wants a higher-paying job.
3. Many retail stores send out catalogs.
4. Keep expense receipts for tax time.
5. Karen helped her patient into a chair.
6. The travel agent reserved my seats six weeks in advance.
7. The auto-body shop replaced the passenger door on my car.
8. The physician's assistant prepared Anton for the tests.
9. The lab technician needed four blood samples from her.
10. Derek slid another disk into the disk drive.

Underline the predicate with one line and the indirect object with a broken line. The first one is done for you.

11. The store mailed special customers the advance notice of the sale.
12. Mr. King offered Shane the chance to be the manager of the new store.
13. Filipe gave his instructor the sketches for the new designs.
14. Brad saves his boss money by doing repairs himself.
15. Maria sent the billing office the receipts for her recent sales trip.
16. Jenny handed Mrs. Rather the letters she wanted.
17. The dental assistant showed Nelson the proper way to brush his teeth.
18. Sam tossed Sarah the electrical tape she needed.
19. Monique read her boss the first draft of the report.
20. Tracee found Jerome the wrench he wanted.

LESSON 2.4

Predicate Nominative, Predicate Adjective

Objective   To identify a predicate nominative and a predicate adjective.

A **predicate nominative** is a noun or pronoun that follows a form of the verb *be* and refers to or describes the subject.

<table>
<tr><td colspan="4" align="center">**Forms of *be***</td></tr>
<tr><td>be</td><td>was</td><td>had been</td><td>shall have been</td></tr>
<tr><td>am</td><td>were</td><td>will be</td><td>being (with auxiliary verbs)</td></tr>
<tr><td>are</td><td>has been</td><td>shall be</td><td></td></tr>
<tr><td>is</td><td>have been</td><td>will have been</td><td></td></tr>
</table>

How do you know if a sentence has a predicate nominative?

1   Read the sentence.

2   Look for a form of *be*. (If the predicate is not a form of *be,* look instead for a direct object.)

3   If the predicate is a form of *be,* ask ''what'' or ''who'' after the predicate. If the answer is a noun, it is a predicate nominative.

EXAMPLE

Mr. Boski is the new boss.

1   Read the sentence.

2   *is* is the predicate, a form of *be*.
Who *is?*
Mr. Boski is.
Mr. Boski is the subject.

3   *Mr. Boski is* what?
Mr. Boski is *boss*.
boss is the predicate nominative—a noun that follows a form of *be* and refers back to the subject.
Mr. Boski and *boss* are the same person.

A **predicate adjective** is an adjective that follows a linking verb and refers to or describes the subject.

A **linking verb** is any form of *be* or any other verb that links the noun, pronoun, or adjective with the subject. A linking verb does not show action.

Other Linking Verbs			
appear	continue	look	smell
be	feel	remain	sound
become	grow	seem	taste

How do you know if a sentence has a predicate adjective?

1 Read the sentence.

2 Look for a linking verb. (If the predicate is not a linking verb, look instead for a direct object.)

3 If the predicate is a linking verb, ask "what" or "how" after the predicate. If the answer is an adjective, it is the predicate adjective.

EXAMPLE

Anne seems anxious about the interview.

1 Read the sentence.

2 The predicate is *seems,* a linking verb.
Who *seems?*
Anne seems.
Anne is the subject.

3 *Anne seems* what?
Anne seems *anxious.*
anxious is the predicate adjective—an adjective that follows a linking verb and describes the subject.

EXAMPLE

The coffee sample tastes bitter.

1 Read the sentence.

2 *tastes* is the predicate, a linking verb.
What *tastes?*
sample tastes.
sample is the subject.

3   *sample tastes* how?
sample tastes *bitter*.
bitter is the predicate adjective—it describes the taste of the sample.

Note that linking verbs like *taste, feel,* and *smell* can also be action verbs. The kind of verb depends on its use. Here, *taste, feel,* and *smell* are action verbs.

- The chef *tasted* the sample. *tasted* what? tasted the *sample. (sample* is the direct object, not a predicate adjective.) (The chef performed the action of tasting.)
- He *feels* the leg for any evidence of broken bones. (the action of feeling)
- Brian *smelled* the new paint as soon as he walked into the office. (the action of smelling)

Pronouns as predicate nominatives will be treated in Lesson 2.5.

PRACTICE

Tell whether the underlined predicate is A, an action verb, or L, a linking verb. The first one is done for you.

1. Marcus <u>felt</u> the drawing to see if the ink had dried.   <u>A</u>
2. Six workmen <u>feel</u> sick.   ___
3. Dawn <u>tested</u> the melon to see if it was ripe.   ___
4. Ms. Mason's picture <u>appeared</u> in the company newsletter.   ___
5. The fresh air <u>smelled</u> good to Jan, who had been in the lab all day.   ___
6. Bethany <u>looked</u> excited about the new project.   ___
7. Kadeem <u>became</u> a supervisor last month.   ___
8. Matt <u>looked</u> at the X rays before showing them to the doctor.   ___
9. Calculators <u>have become</u> very inexpensive.   ___
10. The technicians <u>remained</u> optimistic even though some of the test results were bad.   ___

Underline the predicate nominative or predicate adjective and draw an arrow to the word to which it refers. The first one is done for you.

11. I was the first <u>person</u> to complete the application.

12. They are your co-workers on this project.

13. Mr. Fritz felt bad about losing Michelle to another company.

14. The bank teller seemed doubtful about my identification.

15. The new air conditioner was powerful enough to keep the whole office cool.

16. The house appears smaller than it did in the blueprints.

17. Dolores remained afraid to try the new computer.

18. The conference room smelled better with the windows opened.

19. Profits grew smaller as inflation increased.

20. The engine sounded fine after the tune-up.

Cases of Pronouns

Objective   To learn the three cases of pronouns and to use them correctly.

There are three cases, or forms, of pronouns: *nominative case, objective case,* and *possessive case*. The correct case of a pronoun must be used. The following chart will explain the cases.

	Nominative Case	Objective Case	Possessive Case
Pronouns	I, we, you, he, she, it, they	me, us, you, him, her, it, them	my, mine, our, ours, your, yours, his, her, hers, its, their, theirs
Explanation	Word is subject of the action of the predicate or follows a verb of being (am, is, are, was, were, be, been) as a predicate nominative.	Word is direct or indirect object of the action of the predicate or the object of a preposition.	Word shows ownership.
Example	*He* called the office. The callers were *they*.	The boss called *her*. The caller is one of *us*. I gave them the message.	The operator placed *my* call.

♦ Trouble Spots

1. *Compound subjects:* Sometimes the nominative-case pronoun may sound wrong to you; but if the word is a subject, the nominative case is correct.

> **EXAMPLE**
>
> Tameka and she went out to lunch. (NOT Tameka and her . . .)
>
> He and I went out to lunch. (NOT Him and me . . .)

2. *After a verb of being:* Sometimes the nominative case sounds wrong after a predicate that is a verb of being, but it is correct, because it refers to the subject.

> **EXAMPLE**
>
> It is I. (NOT It is me.)
>
> It was he. (NOT It was him.)

3. *Compound objects:* Sometimes the objective case may sound wrong to you; but if the word is an object, it must be the objective case.

> **EXAMPLE**
>
> It was sent to her and me. (NOT It was sent to she and I.)
>
> They sent me and them to the convention. (NOT They sent I and they . . .)

> **PRACTICE**

Underline the correct pronoun. Write the case of the correct pronoun on the line. The first one is done for you.

1. Omar is getting prices on a new computer for (we, <u>us</u>).   objective _____

2. The bank arranged a home equity loan for my husband and (I, me).   _____

3. A manufacturer's representative showed (them, they) how to use the new copy machine.   _____

4. The business school where (she, her) and I work has a very good system for making lunches.   _____

5. The printer had the T-shirt order ready for (I, me) in less than two days.   _____

6. The best sales team of the week was you and (I, me).   _____

7. Kristi and (she, her) are both nurse's aides.   _____

8. The health department inspected Jordan and (me, my) restaurant.   _____

9. It was (she, her) and (I, me) who convinced them to bring in a new bookkeeper.   _____

10. (Us, We) and Jerry submitted sketches for the new design.   _____

LESSON 2.6

Phrases

Objective   To identify a phrase in a sentence and tell the kind of phrase.

A **phrase** is a group of words that does not have a subject or a predicate. A phrase acts as one part of speech—a noun, an adjective, or an adverb.

1. As you learned in Lesson 1.16, a *prepositional phrase* is a preposition with its object (a noun or pronoun) and any words between the preposition and its object. It can be used as an adjective or an adverb. (Review the list of prepositions on page 38.

EXAMPLE

The original was left *in the copy machine*.
in the copy machine is an adverb phrase; tells *where* the original was left.

The instruments *on the table* should go into the autoclave.
on the table is an adjective phrase; tells *which instruments*.

2. An *infinitive* is the present tense of a verb preceded by the word *to*—to type, to buy, to work.
An *infinitive phrase* is an infinitive with any modifying words. It can be used as a noun, adjective, or adverb.

EXAMPLE

Tracy's goal was *to be a legal secretary*.

infinitive—*to be*
infinitive phrase—*to be a legal secretary*
use in sentence—noun; modifies *goal*

Peter went *to buy his lunch*.

infinitive—*to buy*
infinitive phrase—*to buy his lunch*
use in sentence—adverb; modifies *went*

A refrigerator is a device *to cool foods*.

infinitive—*to cool*
infinitive phrase—*to cool foods*
use in sentence—adjective; modifies *device*

3. A *participial phrase* is a participle (past or present) and its related words. It is used as an adjective and can come before or after the noun or pronoun it modifies.

EXAMPLE

That man *running for the elevator* is my partner.

participle—*running*
participial phrase—*running for the elevator*
modifies—*man*

EXAMPLE

Running for the elevator, I dropped my lunch.

participle—*running*
participial phrase—*running for the elevator*
modifies—*I*

Note: Sometimes a person might write:

Running for the elevator, my lunch dropped.

The phrase does not have a word to modify. The lunch was not running for the elevator. Make sure it is clear what the phrase is modifying. An introductory participial phrase should, logically, modify the subject.

4. A *gerund* is the present participle of a verb and is used as a noun—testing, repairing, processing. A *gerund phrase is* a gerund and its related words. It is used as a noun.

EXAMPLE

Running your own business is a challenge.

gerund—*running*
gerund phrase—*running your own business*
Phrase is used as the subject of the sentence.

EXAMPLE

Keith likes *salvaging old cars*.

gerund—*salvaging*
gerund phrase—*salvaging old cars*
Phrase is used as the direct object of the sentence.

PRACTICE

A phrase is underlined. Identify the kind of phrase. The first one is done for you.

1. Lending money is a loan officer's job.   Gerund phrase

2. Vinnie hopes to sell his condo soon.   _____

3. Saving her document, Halima erased it instead.   _____

4. Nita trained to be a nurse's aide at St. Joseph's Hospital.   _____

5. Frank enjoys planning sales campaigns.   _____

6. The vacation increasing most in popularity is a cruise.   _____

7. Sandy never before wanted to work in the travel business.   _____

8. Hector is becoming interested in culinary arts.   _____

9. My brother helped me to find this job.   _____

10. Jamal is thinking about starting his own bookkeeping business.   _____

On the blank, write the phrase asked for. The first one is done for you.

11. Left in charge of the display booth, Danielle decided to try some of her own ideas.

   Participial: Left in charge of the display booth.

12. Repairing the transmission took Barney all day.

    Gerund: _____

13. To learn computer programming is Amber's dream.

    Infinitive: _____

14. The pipes under the sink are the ones that need fixing.

    Prepositional: _____

15. Sarah was caught listening to the radio.

    Participial: _____

16. You must promise to finish the job today.

    Infinitive: _____

17. Tim agreed to submit a bid for the contract.

    Infinitive: _____

18. Learning shorthand is the reason Roxanne went to business school.

    Gerund: _____

19. The "enter" key is right above the "shift" key.

    Prepositional: _____

20. The person selling the most ads will receive a bonus.

    Participial: _____

LESSON 2.7

Clauses

Objective   To identify independent and dependent clauses.

A **clause** is a part of a sentence. The clause contains a subject and a predicate.

A sentence can be one of three types:

1. *Simple sentence*—one subject, one predicate

EXAMPLE

I need six copies.
Brian repairs computers.

2. *Compound sentence*—two or more simple sentences joined by a conjunction or punctuation

EXAMPLE

Jenny got up earlier, but she still missed her bus.
Carlo became a mechanic, and he enjoys his work.
The orders arrived in the mail; we sold them immediately.

3. *Complex sentence*—one independent clause and one or more dependent clauses joined by a subordinating conjunction

EXAMPLE

I should get a good job *when I graduate.*

To understand what a complex sentence is, you need to understand independent and dependent clauses.
An *independent clause* can stand alone as a simple sentence.

EXAMPLE

You can expect to get a good job when you have your degree.
Independent clause: *you can expect to get a good job*

1 subject—*you*

2 predicate—*can expect*

3 complete thought

A *dependent clause* cannot stand alone as a simple sentence. The clause begins with a *subordinating conjunction* that prevents it from expressing a complete thought.

Subordinating Conjunctions			
after	because	so that	when
although	before	than	whenever
as	for	that	where
as if	if	though	whereas
as long as	once	till	wherever
as soon as	since	unless	whether
as though	so	until	while

Independent clause: Elena became a secretary.

Dependent clauses: *Because* Elena became a secretary
Since Elena became a secretary
Although Elena became a secretary

The dependent clauses leave you waiting for the rest of the thought—the thought is hanging, incomplete. A dependent clause must be in a sentence with an independent clause.

EXAMPLE

Because Elena became a secretary, she learned to use a word processor.

Since Elena became a secretary, she has been promoted twice.

Although Elena became a secretary, she still has an interest in nursing.

PRACTICE

Identify the clause as *Independent* or *Dependent*. The first one is done for you.

1. Until David is a licensed plumber. _____Dependent_____

2. If you are interested in the travel industry. _____

3. Tara is training to be a bank teller. _____

4. Tony received a refund on his income taxes. _____

5. Although you bought a new freezer. _____

6. Walking is a good exercise for general fitness. _____

7. Before I became a dental assistant. _____

8. Computers are important to every kind of job. _____

9. Whenever Al bought his supplies from that dealer. _____

10. A floppy disk is just a sheet of special plastic with a coating of magnetic material. _____

Underline the independent clause with one line and the dependent clause with two lines. The first one is done for you.

11. Jean flew to the conference <u>so she would have more time in New York</u>.

12. Before Fred became a motorcycle technician, he was a motorcycle salesman.

13. My office bought a new copy machine so we could process forms more quickly.

14. Although insurance is a big business, we try to keep our services on a personal level.

15. The secretary will send you your test results as soon as they come in.

16. Jackie had to redo the copies because they came out too light.

17. Unless you place your order eight weeks in advance, we cannot guarantee delivery.

18. Chris became a welder, for he likes working with his hands.

19. Kate is taking a vacation after she graduates from secretarial school.

20. As long as you make your payments on time, you will have a good credit rating.

3

Refining Sentences

Subject-Predicate Agreement

Objective   To make the verb that is the predicate agree with the noun that is the subject in number and person.

♦ **Simple Subject**

Nouns have singular and plural forms.

EXAMPLE

Singular	Plural
woman	women
paper	papers
child	children
search	searches

The verb that is a predicate must agree in number with the noun that is its subject. That means a singular verb is used with a singular noun and a plural verb is used with a plural noun.

EXAMPLE

Singular	Plural
woman types	women type
paper is	papers are
child grows	children grow
search continues	searches continue

It is interesting that regular nouns add an *-s* in the *plural*, and regular verbs add an *-s* in the *singular*. Therefore, an *-s* added to a verb does *not* make the verb plural.

If the subject of a sentence is a pronoun, then the verb that is the predicate must agree in *person* and *number* with the pronoun. The third-person-singular pronouns use the singular form of the verb, while the others use the plural.

	Singular	Plural
1st person	I type.	We type.
2nd person	You type.	You type.
3rd person	He, she, it types.	They type.

Here are the forms of the verb *be:*

	Singular	Plural
	I am.	We are.
	You are.	You are.
	He, she, it is.	They are.

♦ Compound Subject

If the nouns of a compound subject are joined by *and* or *not only . . . but,* the verb is plural unless the compound is thought of as one thing.

EXAMPLE

Scott *and* Ramon *are* medical assistants.

Pens *and* pencils *go* in the top drawer.

Not only Charles *but also* Juan work in this office.

But: Bacon and eggs *is* a high-cholesterol meal.

If a singular noun and a plural noun are joined by *or* or *nor,* the verb should agree with the number of the noun closest to the verb.

EXAMPLE

Neither John nor his *brothers sell* insurance.

Computers or a *word processor is* used.

◆ Collective Nouns

Collective nouns are nouns that name a group.

EXAMPLE

mob	committee	family
class	audience	team
jury	faculty	staff

If the collective noun is considered as one unit, it takes a singular verb. If the *individuals* of the collective noun are considered, it takes a plural verb.

EXAMPLE

The *committee decides* who is hired. (the committee as a unit)

But: The *committee were* going to different restaurants for lunch. (individuals)

◆ Unusual Cases

1. These are always considered as singular:

    time of day: One o'clock *is* the time for lunch.

    a sum of money: Twenty-eight dollars *is* the hourly rate.

    organizations: The United Nations *hires* many interpreters.

    titles: The Yellow Pages *contains* many company names.

2. If a prepositional phrase follows a subject, be sure the verb agrees with the noun that is the subject and not the noun in the phrase.

EXAMPLE

The *package* of pencils *is* on the desk.

The *members* of the union *want* to strike.

3. In questions or in sentences that begin with *There,* the predicate comes before the subject, and noun-verb agreement must be checked.

EXAMPLE

There is one opening in my office. (one opening *is*)

There were three applications for the job. (three applications *were*)

Are two people enough for the project? (two people *are*)

Does one secretary do all this work? (one secretary *does do*)

PRACTICE

Underline the correct verb. The first one is done for you.

1. Technicians (tests, <u>test</u>).
2. Wires (runs, run).
3. Shop (hire, hires).
4. Foremen (treats, treat).
5. Employment agencies (pays, pay).
6. I (go, goes).
7. Jolie and Kendra (programs, program).
8. Eric (repairs, repair).
9. Ravar (type, types).
10. Secretaries (chooses, choose).
11. The usual dosage (is, are) 100 milligrams twice a day.
12. The tenants in my building (is, are) going to petition the landlord for better locks on the doors.
13. The electric company (has, have) offered its customers new, efficient lightbulbs at half price.
14. The salespeople in the computer store (works, work) for a commission.
15. You can (takes, take) your vacation any time from June 1 to August 1.
16. My medical insurance (covers, cover) all hospital laboratory tests.
17. Unions (was, were) started to get better conditions for workers.

18. I (pay, pays) $20 a week to park my car in a garage.

19. My brother (has, have) been looking for a job for a year and a half.

20. Many jobs in the 21st century (is, are) going to be in the service industries.

LESSON 3.2

Punctuation

Objective   To use correct punctuation in sentences.

Punctuation is the process of putting **punctuation marks** in a sentence.

Punctuation marks separate sentences and separate the parts of a sentence so the meaning is clear.

End punctuation:	period .
	exclamation point !
	question mark ?
Internal punctuation:	comma ,
	semicolon ;
	colon :
	dash —
	parentheses ( )
	hyphen -
	quotation marks " "

♦ End Punctuation

In Lesson 2.2, you learned the different kinds of sentences and the end punctuation mark that each requires.

Declarative—period:	July 4 is a national holiday.
Imperative—period:	Send announcements to all the branch offices.
Interrogative—question mark:	Have you set up the vacation schedule yet?
Exclamatory—exclamation point:	We won the account!

◆ Internal Punctuation

1. Comma

A comma is used to separate items in a series; the clauses of a compound sentence; introductory words, phrases, and clauses; parenthetical expressions; dates and addresses; some appositives; direct quotations; and direct address.

That is a long list, but many of them are placed naturally as you pause in your thoughts or reading.

Series. Put a comma after each item of a list of three or more items that is written in a sentence. (Read the following example to yourself, and notice how you pause where the commas are.)

EXAMPLE

I placed an order for *pens, pencils, markers,* and *grease pencils.*

Compound sentence. Put a comma before the conjunction that joins the clauses of a compound sentence.

EXAMPLE

Gavin finished his apprenticeship, and then he became a licensed electrician.

Introductory words, phrases, and clauses. Put a comma after all phrases and clauses that begin a sentence.

EXAMPLE

Yes, we ordered the new fax machine. (word)

Of the three samples, I like the middle one best. (phrase)

On the plane to Chicago, she finished reading the report. (two phrases)

Hearing the buzzer, Mark knew the coffee was ready. (phrase)

When you finish checking the wiring, please call me. (clause)

As you can see, the comma comes right before the subject of the sentence (the independent clause). If you read each sentence, you will probably find that you pause naturally at each place where a comma should be. This will help you in knowing where to place a comma.

Parenthetical expressions.   Put a comma before and after expressions that are not necessary to the meaning of the sentence, such as *of course, in fact,* or *for example.*

EXAMPLE

Health insurance, *of course,* is offered to every employee.

A secretary could work, *for example,* for a doctor, in a bank, or in a court.

Dates and addresses.   Put a comma between the day and year in a date. If the date is in the middle of a sentence, put commas before and after the year. No comma is used after just a month and day.

EXAMPLE

July 4, 1776

I joined this company on December 27, 1950, when I was 18 years old.

Thanksgiving is on November 28 this year.

Put a comma between city and state or before and after the state if it is in the middle of a sentence.

EXAMPLE

Ames, Iowa

Luisa lived in Atlanta, Georgia, before she moved to Pittsburgh.

Appositives will be discussed in Lesson 3.4. *Direct address* and *direct quotations* will be discussed in Lesson 3.5.

2. Semicolon

A semicolon is used to separate the independent clauses of a compound sentence when a conjunction is not used.

EXAMPLE

Tomorrow is a holiday; you can leave early today.

3. Colon

A colon is used to indicate a list or series if there are no words like *like* or *such as*. Use an independent clause before a colon.

EXAMPLE

Food-service jobs are available in many places: schools, hospitals, factories, and large office buildings.

But: You could work in a cafeteria in many places, such as a school, a hospital, or a factory.

4. Dash

Put a dash in place of a comma or semicolon when a stronger break is needed or to avoid confusion with other commas.

EXAMPLE

My boss requested—in fact, he demanded—that I retype the letter.

Kelly was excited—very excited—about the job in California.

5. Parentheses

Put parentheses around material that is not necessary to the sentence. Parentheses are used where commas might be used, but parentheses are stronger.

EXAMPLE

The colors of the flag (red, white, and blue) were repeated in the table decorations.

6. Hyphen

Put a hyphen between the parts of most compound words and between the parts of a word that must be divided at the end of a line.

EXAMPLE

A six-page report will probably require extra postage to mail.

An operator's manual must contain detailed instructions for the machine's use.

There were twenty-five applicants for the job.

Quotation marks will be discussed in Lesson 3.5.

PRACTICE

Insert the proper end punctuation. The first one is done for you.

1. Hurray! We won the new contract!
2. Can that paint job be finished on Friday
3. Court will come to order
4. I have to fast 14 hours so I can have a cholesterol test
5. Do you know the phone number for the IRS
6. Congratulations, you did it
7. Where did I put that disk
8. Sherry is going to night school to learn COBOL
9. Please, hold that elevator
10. Gordon plays handball after work

Insert commas in the proper places. The first one is done for you.

11. Tiffany, Jed, and Allen work on the fourth floor.
12. No that is not what I ordered.
13. Before you turn off the computer remove the disk from the disk drive.
14. In that catalog the price was $4.94 a dozen.
15. My brother is an orderly and I am a nurse's aide.
16. That fender will have to be sanded primed and then painted.
17. Instead of dinner would you like to have lunch?
18. After I finish with the doctor I would like to make an appointment to have my teeth cleaned.
19. My car unfortunately needs a new muffler.
20. Your income taxes of course depend on how much you earn.

Insert a semicolon or a colon. The first one is done for you.

21. Many remedies are suggested for a cold: soup, juice, water, aspirin, rest, hot showers, and so on.
22. The first thing you should do is type a résumé you should then send it to as many companies as you can.

23. This job has several benefits medical insurance, profit-sharing, a pension plan, and life insurance.

24. I can't drive my car this week the engine is being overhauled.

25. Everyone needs to avoid foods high in fat bacon, butter, cream, some cheese, eggs, fried foods, and potato chips, for example.

Insert the required punctuation. The first one is done for you.

26. Parentheses: We are open 9:00 A.M. to 5:00 P.M. weekdays (Monday through Friday).

27. Hyphen: He made reservations for a two week vacation.

28. Two dashes: When you are ready and I hope it's soon you can finish that typing.

29. Parentheses: All employees men and women are treated equally.

30. Hyphen: Crystal is a medical assistant in a family oriented doctor's office.

LESSON 3.3

Dangling Participles, Misplaced Modifiers

Objective To place participial phrases and modifiers so the meaning of the sentence is clear.

If phrases and modifiers are not near the word they modify, the meaning of the sentence can be incorrect or even silly.

A *dangling participle* (or participial phrase) does not modify any word in the sentence because the sentence was written incorrectly.

EXAMPLE

Dangling: *Visiting the stockroom,* the tour of the factory ended.
      (The *tour* was not visiting the stockroom.)

Correct: Visiting the stockroom, the applicants ended the tour of the factory. (*Applicants* did the *visiting.*)

Dangling: Jack broke his arm falling off the ladder.
      (The *arm* did not fall off the ladder.)

Correct: Jack broke his arm when he fell off the ladder.

Or: Falling off the ladder, Jack broke his arm.

A *misplaced modifier* is a word, phrase, or clause that seems to modify the wrong word. The modifier must be moved to a place in the sentence where it is clear what word is being modified.

1. *Word:* Look at what the word *only* can do to this sentence.

   Only Mitchell can save three documents.
   (*Meaning:* Mitchell is the only one who can do it.)

   Mitchell can *only* save three documents.
   (*Meaning:* He can save the documents but not print them.)

   Mitchell can save *only* three documents.
   (*Meaning:* He cannot save four or five documents.)

2. *Phrase:* Changing the placement of the phrase changes the sentence.

   A woman *from my office* ordered new chairs.

   A woman ordered new chairs *from my office*.

3. *Clause:* The clause must be near the word it modifies.

   Misplaced: The people in that office decided to collect money for children while they are on their break.
   (The children are not on their break.)

   Clear: The people in that office decided that, while they are on their break, they will collect money for children.

Always read over your written work to be sure modifiers are placed for clear and correct meaning.

PRACTICE

Rewrite the sentence to eliminate the dangling participle or misplaced modifier. The first one is done for you.

1. In the refrigerator, Miguel saw his lunch.

   Miguel saw his lunch in the refrigerator.

   _____

2. Wanting to avoid a strike, a new union contract was drawn up by the negotiating committee.

   _____

   _____

3. The computer and the printer with its monitor cost $2,000.

   _____

   _____

4. Be sure to put that letter on your way out in the IN box.

_____

_____

5. Driving to work, the car had a flat tire.

_____

_____

6. Rosa's patient, Mrs. Amano, had X rays taken while she was at lunch.

_____

_____

7. After typing a letter, your boss should check it for errors.

_____

_____

8. Recovering from flu, the doctor told Anne to stay in bed three days.

_____

_____

9. Looking in the operator's manual, the start button seems to be the red one.

_____

_____

10. The pharmacist asked Mario to lock the drugstore every night during his vacation.

_____

_____

LESSON 3.4

Appositives

Objective   **To identify an appositive and to set it off correctly with commas.**

An **appositive** is a noun or phrase that explains or renames the noun or pronoun immediately before it.

EXAMPLE

The teller, *Mr. Forbes,* had me endorse the check again.

(The appositive is *Mr. Forbes.* It tells the name of the teller, but it is not information necessary to the sentence. So it is set off by commas.)

My friend *Suzanne* became an X ray technician.

(The appositive is *Suzanne.* It tells which friend. There is more than one friend, so *Suzanne* is necessary to the sentence. It is not set off by commas.)

My sister, Eva, is a home health care aide.

(*Eva* is set off by commas. It is not necessary to the sentence because you have only one sister.)

Ben works at 125 Fifth Avenue, the building with all the flags.

(The address is enough to identify the building. The rest is extra information, so a comma is used.)

The popular children's story *Dino* sells very well.

The color grey is common for computer hardware.

(No commas since *Dino* and *grey* are necessary to the sentences.)

Using an appositive can make writing more clear and concise. Using an appositive can combine two sentences into one.

EXAMPLE

Two Sentences:

Two applicants are equally qualified for the job. The applicants are Tonya and Christine.

One Sentence with an Appositive:

Two applicants, Tonya and Christine, are equally qualified for the job.

PRACTICE

Underline the appositive. The first one is done for you.

1. I have wanted this career, <u>computer programming</u>, since I was 12 years old.

2. Pilar's apartment, a one-room efficiency, rents for $390 a month.

3. The main speaker, Senator Jones, is held up in traffic.

4. The second edition of his book *Career Options* was published in 1990.

5. My mother, Angela McGuinness, retired last week.

6. His assistant Sherry is on vacation.

7. Today, Friday, is an important day in the company's history.

8. The salesman Sam Cooper has the highest sales this month.

9. Matthew's favorite suit, the gray pinstripe, is at the cleaner's.

10. Tyrone's brother Randy had the highest score on the entrance exam.

Insert commas around the appositive if you think the meaning of the sentence would be clear without the appositive. Explain your choice of commas or no commas. The first one is done for you.

11. Her boss, Wayne Chong, asked her if she could work overtime.
    Commas around Wayne Chong because most people only have one
    boss—the meaning would still be clear without Wayne Chong.

12. His friend Rob is going to be an avionics technician.

    _____

    _____

13. The head teller Ms. Nunes was promoted to manager.

    _____

    _____

14. His first book *Repairing Your Own Computer* is out of print.

    _____

    _____

15. Rita Mae has four brothers and two sisters; her sister Nicole is in the Navy.

    _____

    _____

Rewrite the two sentences as one sentence with an appositive.

16. Brian's hobby became his career. His hobby was fixing old radios.

    _____

    _____

17. The dental assistant does not work on Tuesday. The dental assistant is Shelley Rogers.

    _____

    _____

18. The last day for submitting next year's budget is tomorrow. Tomorrow is Thursday.

_____

_____

19. My favorite typist is leaving for another job. My favorite typist is Brandy.

_____

_____

20. That computer monitor is out for servicing. It is a color monitor.

_____

_____

LESSON 3.5

Direct Address and Quotes

Objective   To recognize words used in direct address and to use the correct punctuation.

When you speak to someone, you often call him or her by name or title. In writing, the name or title is set off by commas because it is extra—it is not necessary to the meaning of the sentence. The name or title is said to be in *direct address.*

EXAMPLE

Mr. Gordon, the doctor will see you now.

Your appointment, *Anne,* was last Tuesday.

I will read the last testimony for you, *your honor.*

Diana, have you finished that typing?

If the conversation is quoted as the exact words of a person, then it must also have quotation marks. The punctuation of the quotation goes inside the quotation marks.

EXAMPLE

''Mr. Gordon,'' said the receptionist, ''the doctor will see you now.''

(Note that the comma and the period go *inside* the quotation marks.)

"Your appointment, Anne, was last Tuesday," Anne's mother said.

(Note that the period after *Tuesday* becomes a comma when the speaker follows it.)

The court stenographer was heard to say, "I will read the last testimony for you, your honor."

The supervisor asked, "Diana, have you finished that typing?"

(Note that the question mark goes *inside* the quotation marks.)

PRACTICE

Insert commas and quotation marks where needed. The first one is done for you.

1. "Are you familiar with this model refrigerator, Dion?" asked Mr. Fortin.
2. Mai I need this finished by 3 o'clock.
3. When you are ready to start painting the pickup Fabin check with me about the color.
4. Mrs. Yarina said to me When the service rep shows up Carol send him to my office.
5. Bite down on the film Will and I'll take the X ray.
6. I heard the traffic reporter say Avoid the Tenth Street Bridge because of roadwork.
7. That estimate she said is much too high.
8. Ladies and gentlemen we have a new supervisor he announced.
9. Stand when the judge comes in the lawyer whispered to his client.
10. The nurse promised This won't hurt.

4

Paragraph Structure

The Paragraph

Objective   To understand the structure of a paragraph and to identify a topic sentence and a summary sentence.

A **paragraph** is a group of sentences that explain or describe one topic.

The purpose of learning about parts of speech, sentences, and punctuation is to be able to communicate clearly and correctly. The writing most people do is notes or letters. Some people earn a living by writing articles or books. Whatever the purpose of the writing, it should be easy for the reader to understand and follow.

The first sentence of a paragraph is often the *topic sentence,* the sentence that tells what the paragraph is about. Some writers might have a special reason for putting the topic sentence in a different place in the paragraph.

Other sentences in the paragraph are the *detail sentences* or *supporting sentences.* They explain and describe the main topic in a logical way.

The last sentence is often a *summary sentence.* It restates the topic of the paragraph and its explanation in one sentence.

EXAMPLE

The following is a paragraph from an article on effective speaking.

A big part of effective voice control stems from inward sincerity. You are not going to be very convincing if you are not sincere. Say what you mean, and mean what you say. If you are genuinely interested in what you are talking about, your enthusiasm becomes contagious. A good salesman knows his product and likes his product, and his speaking manner reflects this attitude.

The underlined sentence is the *topic sentence;* it tells you that the paragraph is about the effect of sincerity on voice control.

The next three sentences *explain* sincerity and how it affects speech.

The last sentence is the *summary sentence;* it restates the effect of sincerity on speaking.

Think of this pattern as you write any paragraph so your reader will get the message you are sending.

PRACTICE

Read the paragraph and underline the topic sentence. The first one is done for you.

1. Senior citizens don't have to run marathons to reap the benefits of physical fitness. Brisk walking, swimming, and simple weight lifting benefit people at any age. Recent studies show that even leisure activities—gardening and bowling, for instance—burn off calories and help maintain overall fitness. What's most important, say experts, is to find an enjoyable activity, exercise on a regular basis, and consult with a physician before you leap into a program—regardless of your previous athletic stature.

2. Always keep the recommended tire pressure in all your tires, including the spare. On some vehicles, the recommended front and rear tire pressures will be different. A sticker on the tire or your car's owner's manual will tell you the recommended air pressure. Underinflation can cause tires to overheat, damaging the tires. It can also reduce tire life, cause the car to handle poorly, and reduce gas mileage. Overinflation affects tire wear and makes the tire more likely to be cut, punctured, or broken by sudden impact. Note: Never inflate a tire unless it is on the car or secured to a tire-mounting machine.

3. Should you consider a welding career? Not many people are aware of the influence welding has upon our lives. There are few things that you touch or depend upon during the day that haven't been made by welding. Wherever two pieces of metal have been fused, a welder has been there. Be it a coffee pot, an automobile, a bicycle, or a spacecraft, all depend upon welding or brazing for their strength and efficiency. In construction, manufacturing, electronics, the nuclear field, and shipbuilding, skilled welders and welding craftsmen are there to build and maintain the machines. Therefore, the welding field is well worth looking into.

4. Ordinary, everyday contact will not give you AIDS. For example, you won't get AIDS just by being near someone who has it. You won't get AIDS from hugging or kissing. The U.S. Public Health Service also tells us you won't get AIDS from flies, mosquitoes, bedbugs, or lice. You won't get it from saliva, sweat, tears, or urine either. You won't get AIDS from clothes or a telephone or a toilet seat. You won't get it by donating blood to a blood center. You won't get it from dishes or glasses, or from using the same desk or word processor, or from sharing an elevator. In other words, you don't have to worry about ordinary living or working with someone who carries HIV.

5. Twenty years ago, the suggestion that a person could be healthier and lengthen his or her life by getting a dog or cat would have been laughed at by most members of the medical community. But research begun in the early 1970s has proven that pets promote both physical and mental well-being. One of the earliest studies in so-called pet therapy was conducted by a British researcher who wished to measure the effects on lonely elderly women of having an animal companion. Each member of one group was given a parakeet, while each in a second group was given a flowering plant. Those with a bird developed a better outlook on life than those with a plant.

LESSON 4.2

Unity of Thought (Sentences That Do Not Belong, Sentences Out of Order)

Objective   To understand unity and order in a paragraph and to identify sentences that are out of order in a paragraph or do not belong.

The sentences in a paragraph must be in order, just like the steps in a computer program. The sentences must all relate to the topic.

EXAMPLE

Read the numbered sentences of the following paragraph.

1. Our Town Bank started a program to train its workers to make customers happy.

2. Tellers are taught to use a person's name and to greet each person promptly.

3. Customer representatives must answer phone calls by the third ring.

4. The bank's employees are shown films to help them understand why a customer might be grumpy and to help them deal with the grumpy customer.

5. If they need to return a customer's call, they must do so within 24 hours.

6. Our Town Bank's employees get three weeks' vacation.

7. The program must be working because Our Town Bank gets about eight customers a week who transfer from other banks.

8. If a bank wants happy customers, it must teach its employees to make the customers happy.

- Sentence 1 is the topic sentence. It tells what the paragraph is about.
- One sentence does not beong. Which is it?
- Sentence 5 is out of order. Where should it be?
- What do you call sentence 8?

PRACTICE

Underline the sentence that does not belong. The first one is done for you.

1. On the behavioral side, exercise reduces stress and depression. It can enhance mental sharpness and improve the quality of sleep. "It's not just physical: it's a psychological mechanism as well. You'll feel better about yourself with exercise," notes Dr. David A. Baron, a clinical director of the National Institute of Mental Health in Bethesda, Maryland. The capital of Maryland is Annapolis. Even more important to older adults, exercise provides opportunities to socialize.

2. Any tire, no matter how well made, may fail. And a new tire is expensive. It could fail because of punctures, impact damage, improper inflation, overloading, or misuse. Tire failure may mean a risk of serious personal injury or property damage. To reduce the chance of tire failure, follow all the safety rules.

3. One of the most popular singing groups is the Beatles. There was a song which became popular quite a few years ago about a boy named Johnny, who could sing only one note. Using only one note is one way to sing, but it soon becomes very monotonous to the listener. Fortunately, monotonous singing is not a major problem in our daily lives; on the other hand, monotonous *speaking* often *is*. Many people converse in a monotonous voice and think nothing of it. Yet, conversation is such an important means of communication that they are doing themselves, not to mention their listeners, a great disservice.

4. There's no doubt about it; it would be difficult not to have fun in New Brunswick, Canada. There's just so much of it around! People have fun at DisneyWorld, too. Friendly people, clean fresh air, wide open spaces and

lots to do. Whether you are camping or staying in motels, at farm vacation homes, bed-and-breakfast places or country inns, you're sure to have a good time.

5. The word *graphic* means "the expression of ideas by lines or marks impressed on a surface." A drawing is a *graphic representation* of a real thing. Drafting, therefore, is a graphic language because it uses *pictures* to communicate thoughts and ideas. Because these pictures can be understood by residents of different nations, drafting is referred to as a "universal language." People in Europe usually learn to speak English in school.

Underline the sentence that is out of order. Put an asterisk (∗) where you think the misplaced sentence should be. The first one is done for you.

6. But when you order your coffee, you clearly hear the voice of an almost unchanged region in your waitress's Cajun accent. St. Martinville, Louisiana, is small-town America but with a big local difference. Its quiet streets, old storefronts, and corner coffee shop are a typical American scene.∗ She speaks Cajun French as well as she speaks English. It is hard to tell—even by her—which is her first language. Local conversations switch from one language to another as easily as her children switch television channels. It's a fact of life in St. Martinville that French is alive and well in many families. But it's also true that television, education, and commercialism have washed out some of the local color in communities in Acadiana.

7. Two dozen health-care organizations—including the American Nurses Association, the National League for Nursing, and the American Academy of Family Physicians—have joined forces to tackle the problem. The coalition has launched a campaign called the Nutrition Screening Initiative (NSI). Its purpose is to promote routine assessment of elderly patients' nutritional status and better nutritional care. Toward that goal, they plan educational efforts to increase health professionals' awareness of the need to do routine nutritional screening. Many older Americans are seriously malnourished.

8. Liga International, also known as the Flying Doctors of Mercy, is a volunteer group based in Santa Ana, California. Since 1935, doctors, nurses, and other medical personnel have been bringing much-needed medical care to rural Mexico. They maintain six clinics in southern Sonora and northern Sinaloa. In moments, they are airborne, en route to Guaymas, Mexico, on the first leg of the monthly trip with Liga. On the first weekend of every month 25 to 30 planes take off for these clinics, each carrying people, medicine, and supplies.

9. The pain in David Rogers' lower jaw was getting worse. It was beginning to interfere with his concentration. The dentist made a thorough examination. Reluctantly, he took time from work to visit the nearest dentist. He even took Rogers' blood pressure. "Your heartbeat sounds irregular to me," he said as he removed the stethoscope. "It may be normal for you, but I think we should check it out before we go any further."

10. A basic truth that tends to get lost in the glitter surrounding the microelectronic revolution is that digital devices—clocks, calculators, computers, etc.—are nothing more than tools to help people do a job. The pencil is a useful tool; the screwdriver is a useful tool; the computer is a useful tool. Nothing more. Years ago, you might have seen a bank clerk accidentally write down your $1,000 deposit as $100. Did anybody then call this "pencil error"? No. The responsibility belonged to the teller, not the tool. Today, if a bank statement cheats you out of $900 that way, you know what the clerk is sure to say: "It was computer error." Nonsense. The computer is reporting nothing more than what the clerk typed into it.

LESSON 4.3

Kinds of Paragraphs

Objective   To identify various kinds of paragraphs.

There are several kinds of paragraphs. The kind depends on the purpose of the paragraph.

1. Descriptive paragraph—describes something.
2. How-to paragraph—gives directions for doing something.
3. Comparison paragraph—shows how two things are alike.
4. Contrasting paragraph—shows how two things are different.
5. Cause-and-effect paragraph—shows how causes result in certain effects.
6. Persuasive paragraph—convinces someone to think the way the writer does.

The following is a *descriptive* paragraph.

> The courtroom had a simple and modern appearance. The walls and ceilings were painted gray. The table and chair frames were a light brown wood. The chairs and carpets were a matching blue wool. The judge sat at a black desk on a raised platform. The partitions that separated the jury and spectator sections from the rest of the room were painted white. It all combined to create a calming atmosphere.

The first sentence is the topic sentence—it states that a courtroom will be described. The rest of the sentences give details about the appearance of the courtroom. The last sentence sums up the atmosphere created.

This paragraph is very different from what a lawyer might write to persuade a jury that a person is innocent or guilty.

It is very different from the directions that the judge might give the jury on how they should reach their decision.

You must keep the purpose of your writing clearly in mind when you write a paragraph.

PRACTICE

Identify the kind of paragraph. The first one is done for you.

1. How-to paragraph

To clean the coils of an air conditioner, use a garden hose with a nozzle. Use the strongest solid stream of water. Direct the water into the coil in the direction opposite to the air flow. Air flow direction is into the condenser box. At first the water will dribble through the coil. Eventually, the water will flood through, indicating it's clean.

2. _____

People have developed drawing along two distinct lines, using each form for a different purpose. Artistic drawing is mainly concerned with the expression of real or imagined ideas of a cultural nature. On the other hand, technical drawing is concerned with the expression of technical ideas or ideas of a practical nature, and is used in all branches of technical industry.

3. _____

If you and your family are camping, be sure to check for special kids' programs offered at the campground. The two national parks, Kouchibouguac and Fundy, as well as many of the provincial parks in New Brunswick, often have activities especially for young people. Whether you choose arts and crafts, sports, music, games or swimming lessons, you'll be sure to have a lot of fun.

4. _____

Along Bayou Teche, the land is planted in sugar cane and the towns are shaded by large oaks. St. Martinville is here; the Atchafalaya Swamp is not far away. Westward is the Vermilion Bayou and Abbeville with its two town squares and, like all the other places, its language, crawfish, Catholic church, and surrounding farmland. Rice and soybeans are the cash crops on the prairie. Southward to the coast, some farmers double as trappers, harvesting furs from the marshes each winter.

5. _____

Being able to adjust the power allows greater control of the heating rate and aids in keeping nutrients. Research show that with the use of low power, microwave-prepared foods have the same as or more B vitamins, thiamine, riboflavin, pyridoxine, folacin, and vitamin C than foods prepared in usual ways. Because microwave cooking requires less time, vitamins and minerals are spared some of the destruction that normally occurs in baking and roasting.

LESSON 4.4

Transitional Words and Phrases

Objective   To improve paragraph flow by using linking words and phrases.

The sentences and ideas in a paragraph flow one from the other. Some words and phrases make the links, or connections, between the sentences and clauses smoother and more easy to follow. They move the reader along in the writing and may alert them to a change or to a new step or thought.

Some Linking Words and Phrases

but	so	still	even so
therefore	even though	after	since
first, second, third, etc.	for instance	as	while
	consequently	as soon as	however
next	then	for example	now
furthermore	finally	in spite of	later
in fact	because	in addition	meanwhile

EXAMPLE

First, I inserted the disk into the disk drive. *Then* I turned on the computer.

Even though I placed the order early, we *still* ran out of stationery.

Cleanse the spot on the patient's arm with alcohol. *After* that, prepare the syringe.

PRACTICE

Underline the linking words or phrases in these paragraphs. The first word is done for you.

1. There are <u>still</u> other new uses for temporary service. For example, smooth transitions can be achieved when such employees are used during office and plant relocations. In addition, temporaries can be used in jobs during the delays while formal written job descriptions are being drafted. Finally, temporary employees can fill essential jobs until hiring freezes are lifted.

The applications are almost limitless. As a result, temporary service firms and their customer companies are constantly working out flexible cost-saving solutions to complicated staffing and workload problems.

2. In spite of all this, smoking can be conquered. It is true that ex-heroin users have reported that tobacco's grip was harder to break than their drug habit. But 43 million Americans have managed to quit smoking, mostly succeeding on their own. More and more, though, the one-third of all Americans who still smoke are seeking help in antismoking programs. These generally stress that the tobacco habit is a treatable addiction.

    The real key to success, however, lies in the amount of encouragement smokers get from physicians, friends, and relatives. That's what the experts tell us. Without doubt, the benefits of quitting are worth the struggle.

Insert a linking word or phrase between the sentences:

3. Daryl did not like his résumé. _____, he rewrote it.

4. Maggie had an interview for a new job. _____ she has three years' experience, she is sure she will get the job.

5. Many things people use everyday have been welded together. _____, people do not realize the widespread use of welding.

6. As long as my boss is around, everything goes well with the computer. _____ he leaves the office, something breaks down.

7. Marty lives three miles from his job. _____ the distance, he likes to walk to work every day.

5

Refining a Paragraph

Consistent Verb Tenses

Objective   To use verb tenses correctly in a paragraph.

You should remember from the first chapter that the basic verb tenses are present, past, and future. Different tenses can be used in the same paragraph.

EXAMPLE

past { Melissa always wanted to be a dental assistant. When she was a little girl, she examined her friends' teeth. She even brushed their teeth for them. Melissa took good care of her own teeth and read books and articles about dentistry. Now her studies are almost

present { finished. She is ready to graduate and look for a job. Melissa will

future { soon be a dental assistant; she will reach her goal.

In this paragraph, the first four sentences are in the past tense. The next two are present tense, and the last is future tense.

It is logical to move from the past to the present to the future. In the following sentence, the change of tenses is incorrect.

Incorrect: When I went to the storeroom, I get a pen.
              past   present

These sentences are correct.

When I go to the storeroom, I will get a pen.
        present   future

When I went to the storeroom, I got a pen.
        past   past

When I go to the storeroom, I get a pen.
        present   present

A change of tenses in a sentence or in a paragraph must be logical.

past to present

past to future

present to future

Correct: Robert bought a computer and is moving it to his office. (past to present)

Robert bought a computer and will move it to his office. (past to future)

Robert is buying a computer and will move it to his office. (present to future)

Incorrect: Robert is buying a computer and moved it to his office. (present to past)

Robert will buy a computer and moved it to his office. (future to past)

PRACTICE

1. In each blank, write the correct form of the given verb. The first one is done for you.

In his excellent book, *The Corporate Steeplechase,* Srully Blotnick ____advised____ young people not to take a job just *past tense of advise* for the money or the honor, but rather for the enjoyment of doing it. That way, if things work out, they _____ rich and happy. If things do not *future tense of be* work out, they will still be happy. Young Bob McKnight _____ that good advice is very much at the *present tense of think* heart of the company's success. "Best of all, this business is still fun," he _____ . "If I couldn't surf every- *present tense of beam* day, I wouldn't be here."

2. In each blank, write a correct form of the given verb. The first one is done for you. Answers may vary.

Washington, D.C.'s once-proud Union Station <u>has returned</u>   return
to public life. It _____ in October 1988   reopen
after a $120 million, seven-year restoration and redevelopment
effort. Union Station once again _____   contain
Amtrak operations serving some seven million passengers
every year. But the historic turn-of-the-century building also
_____ into a multi-use dining, shopping,   turn
and   entertainment   complex   that   developers   believe
_____ extremely popular with both tourists   be
and people who live in Washington.

L E S S O N   5 . 2

Consistent Person

Objective   To use the correct person in writing.

First Person—Speaker

If you are speaking to someone or writing to someone, the only way you can refer to yourself is to say "I"—or if referring to yourself and someone else together, "we."

   If your name is Norman, you would not say to your friend, "Norman will be on vacation next week." You would say, "I will be on vacation next week." If you and your brother are going together, you would say, "We will be on vacation next week."

Second Person—Spoken To

When speaking to someone else, the other person is "you." Other persons (plural) are also "you."

   Norman would say to Jeremy, "You will like the new office."

   Norman would say to Jeremy and Michael, "You will like the new office."

Third Person—Spoken About

When speaking about someone else, the other people are "he" or "she" (if singular) or "they" (if plural).

Norman would say about Jeremy, "He is perfect for the job."

Norman would say about Jeremy and Michael, "They are perfect for the job."

If you need any more review on the person of pronouns, see Lesson 1.5.

Business, or Formal, Writing

Business writing, sometimes called formal writing, is usually written in the third person. This would include reports, papers, and some letters, for example. The following is written in the third person—there is no "I" or "you."

> Only a small percentage of students taking a drafting course will make drafting a lifetime occupation. However, a thorough understanding of this precise language is necessary for anyone who intends to work in the highly technical manufacturing and construction industries or plans to become a professional engineer. Many more people are required who can read drawings than who can make them. In daily living, a knowledge of drafting is very helpful in understanding house plans; assembly, maintenance, and operating instructions for many manufactured products; and plans and specifications for many hobbies and other leisure activities.

Informal Writing

Writing is called informal if it has "I," "we," and "you" in it. It is more conversational and personal. Some letters would use informal writing, as would some articles or stories.

> Anybody who has tried to write a simple program on a computer—and if you haven't done so, you ought to give it a try—is aware of how hard it can be. The really maddening thing about computers is that they do exactly what you tell them to do. The stupidest typing error you make when entering the program will come back to haunt you, because the computer is too dumb to correct it. This explains why some of the programs we buy for our personal computers produce "computer errors" that seem really ridiculous. The nice thing about the computer revolution we are living in is that computers are becoming democratic. Anybody can have one. Over time, as more people get their hands on computers and learn how they work, we will all understand that the excuse "It was a computer error" is always a little white lie.

The use of *you* and *we* in the above paragraph makes it seem that someone is talking to you.

EXAMPLE

Suppose your name is Alan Garcia and your boss's name is Marcy Linden. You have been promoted to assistant supervisor in your department. Marcy is going to write two notices about the promotion: (1) one to be published in the local papers and (2) another notice to be circulated among the staff. Here is how she might write them.

1. Written formally in third person.

    Ms. Marcy Linden of Simpson Business Products, Inc., has announced the promotion of Mr. Alan Garcia to assistant supervisor in the bookkeeping department. Mr. Garcia was a graduate of Business Tech School and has been with Simpson for three years. The promotion is effective immediately.

2. Written informally in first and second person.

    From the desk of Marcy Linden:

    I am very happy to announce the promotion of Alan Garcia to assistant supervisor in our bookkeeping department. As many of you know, Alan graduated from Business Tech School and has been with us at Simpson for three years. I am sure you join me in wishing Alan success and in supporting him in his new responsibilities.

PRACTICE

Identify the person in which each sentence is written. The first one is done for you.

1. Jody Philips is secretary to Mr. Fritz.   _____third_____

2. I hope I can get that letter done today.   _____

3. You should think about taking night classes.   _____

4. Our department has the best attendance record in the
   company.   _____

5. Did you see the notice about vacation changes?   _____

6. His estimate to fix the disk drive was $74.   _____

7. It is 1 o'clock; we should be getting back to the
   office.   _____

8. Your requisition list did not include computer paper.   _____

9. The doctor said I need to have my cholesterol levels checked. _____

10. Be sure to get a haircut before you go for your interview. _____

11. Write an informal staff memo announcing that Betty Jonas, who has been with the company for 43 years, is going to retire.

_____

_____

_____

_____

_____

_____

_____

_____

_____

_____

_____

_____

12. Write a formal notice to be sent to the newspaper announcing that your company (make up a name) is moving to a new building (make up the old and new addresses). You could mention a building designer, the history of the old building, reasons for moving, and so on.

_____

_____

_____

_____

_____

_____

_____

_____

_____

_____

_____

Consistent Number

Objective   To be consistent with regard to number of pronouns.

Being consistent in number means always to use singular pronouns together and plural pronouns together.

EXAMPLE

Inconsistent: *I* am going to a three-day conference in Boston, and *we* are going to rent a car.

Whether this sentence was written or spoken, the reader or listener would be confused. The first clause uses *I,* and the second clause uses *we.* Who is the other part of *we*?

Consistent: *I* am going to a three-day conference in Boston, and my partner and *I* are going to rent a car.

Now the references are clear.

EXAMPLE

Inconsistent: The *company* said *they* would pay Bob's traveling expenses. *It* would take care of everything but meals.

Company is a collective noun, so it could be understood as singular or plural. Here the meaning should be singular, so singular should be used throughout.

Consistent: The *company* said *it* would pay Bob's traveling expenses. *It* would take care of everything but meals.

PRACTICE

Read the sentence or sentences. Write *Consistent* or *Inconsistent* on the line to describe the use of singular or plural pronouns in the sentence. If it is inconsistent, rewrite the sentence to make it consistent. If this is the case, you may need to change verb forms as well.

1. Stephanie bought a new computer. They paid $1,500 for it.

   Inconsistent

   Stephanie bought a new computer. She paid $1,500 for it.

2. Before I moved into my new apartment, management repainted it for me.

_____

_____

3. The dentist and the technician both told me I should floss more often. He told me to use unwaxed dental floss.

_____

_____

4. The auto-body shop called Cheryl about her car. It would be finished on Tuesday.

_____

_____

5. Lou and I applied for the same job. We are hoping the company needs two people.

_____

_____

6. Dimiso had their computer memory upgraded to 8K. He hopes they will meet his needs.

_____

_____

7. The secretary wrote my name in the appointment book, but they forgot to give me a card.

_____

_____

8. The copy machine was just overhauled. It couldn't possibly be broken again.

_____

_____

9. Leroy reread the statement of the witness to the judge. They has a loud, clear voice.

_____

_____

10. Julio and Melti are home health-care aides. He each has about 10 patients a day.

_____

_____

Active Voice and Passive Voice

Objective   To understand voice with regard to predicates.

The **voice** of a predicate tells how the subject is related to the action of the predicate.

Active voice means the subject performs or performed the action.

EXAMPLE

The dental technician *cleaned* my teeth.

He *faxed* the letter to me.

The mechanic *is replacing* the brake pads on my car.

Passive voice means the subject receives or received the action.

EXAMPLE

My teeth *were cleaned* by the technician.

(The teeth are *receiving* the action of cleaning; they are not doing the cleaning.)

The letter *was faxed* to me by him.

(The letter is *receiving* the action of faxing; it is not doing the faxing.)

The brake pads on my car *are being replaced* by the mechanic.

(The brakes are *receiving* the action of replacing; they are not doing the replacing.)

Form: Verbs in the passive voice have a form of the verb *be* with the past participle of the verb.

	Active voice	Passive voice
clean	cleaned	were cleaned
fax	faxed	was faxed
replace	is replacing	are being replaced

Active voice conveys stronger action than passive voice does. If you want your writing to be more forceful, use active voice whenever you can.

PRACTICE

Identify the voice used in each sentence. Write active or passive on the line. The first one is done for you.

1. The paper jammed in the computer.   <u>   active   </u>

2. The messenger delivered the report.   <u>   </u>

3. Ray charges $10 an hour.   <u>   </u>

4. The pipe was measured at 9 feet 3 inches.   <u>   </u>

5. The checks were shipped by Priority Mail.   <u>   </u>

6. The technician moved my arm to the left for a better
   X ray.   <u>   </u>

7. Interest on home equity loans has dropped to
   7 percent.   <u>   </u>

8. The ad claimed that we would save a lot of money by
   leasing our office machines.   <u>   </u>

9. Coffee pots, bicycles, and airplanes all are welded
   together.   <u>   </u>

10. She made her reservation early enough to get a
    supersaver fare.   <u>   </u>

The following sentences all have verbs in the passive voice. Rewrite each sentence so the verb is in the active voice. The first one is done for you.

11. The computer printer ribbon is changed by Sando about twice a month.

   <u>Sando changes the computer printer ribbon about twice a month.</u>

12. Interviews were held by every company at the job fair.

_____

_____

13. The reports were copied and bound by Trevor's company.

_____

_____

14. Your car's oil should be changed every 3,000 miles.

_____

_____

15. The blood samples for five tests were taken by the medical assistant.

_____

_____

L E S S O N   5 . 5

Avoiding Biased Language

Objective   To be aware of biased language and to avoid using it.

Bias is favoring one thing or person over another.

Biased language would make it seem that one thing or person is better (or worse) than another:

Whites better than minorities.

Men better than women.

Young people better than older people.

Rich better than poor.

Engineers better than clerks.

Gender bias is the bias most often encountered in writing. Masculine pronouns and other terms are used without conscious thought to the fact that the pronouns and terms may be eliminating or putting down women.

Writing can be made neutral by using the following techniques.

1. Use plural pronouns or eliminate pronouns.

EXAMPLE

Biased: An auto *mechanic* has to keep *his* tools in good shape.

Neutral: Auto *mechanics* need to keep *their* tools in good shape. (Singular changed to plural.)

Biased: A nurse's aide should have good rapport with *her* patients.

Neutral: A nurse's aide should have a good rapport with patients. (Eliminate the pronoun.)

2. Repeat the noun.

EXAMPLE

Biased: If a *manager* wants to be respected, *he* should enforce the rules consistently.

Neutral: If a *manager* wanted to be respected, *that manager* should enforce the rules consistently.

Note: If a pronoun refers to a proper name, then it is not biased—it refers to a specific person.

If *Mr. Chang* wants to be respected, *he* should enforce the rules consistently.

If *Mrs. Barros* wants to be respected, *she* should enforce the rules consistently.

3. Change the voice of the verb.

EXAMPLE

Biased: A bank teller *counts* thousands of dollars during her workday. (active voice)

Neutral: Thousands of dollars *are counted* during a bank teller's workday. (passive voice)

4. Use masculine and feminine pronouns together, if no other change can be made or if other changes would be awkward.

EXAMPLE

Biased: A cable TV technician spends a lot of time on ladders, so *he* should not be afraid of heights.

Neutral: A cable TV technician spends a lot of time on ladders, so *he or she* should not be afraid of heights.

5. Use neutral words to replace words that are of themselves one gender or the other.

Biased		Neutral
mailman	—	mail carrier
sisterhood ⎫	—	association
brotherhood ⎭	—	
cleaning woman	—	cleaning person
mankind	—	human race all people women and men

PRACTICE

Rewrite the following sentences to eliminate gender bias. The first one is done for you.

1. A secretary's boss should value her work.

   A boss should value a secretary's work.

   _____

2. The electricians in my company are thinking of forming a group called The Brotherhood of Electricians.

   _____

   _____

3. A nurse's aide must buy her own uniforms.

   _____

   _____

4. A computer repairman earns good money.

   _____

   _____

5. A dental technician wears rubber gloves when she cleans her patient's teeth.

   _____

   _____

6. A career in welding would be a good choice for a man who likes working with his hands.

_____

_____

7. A food-service worker in a school must start her day very early.

_____

_____

8. The legal assistant read his notes to the lawyer.

_____

_____

9. A travel agent tries to get the best rates he can for his customers.

_____

_____

10. A salesgirl looks forward to receiving her commission on sales.

_____

_____

LESSON 5.6

Editing

Objective   To change written work so that its meaning is clear and readable.

The dictionary defines *editing* as "the adapting, changing, or refining of a work to meet a standard or for a particular purpose."

A person who edits is an *editor*. An editor is concerned with the content of a written work, what it says. An editor may sometimes look for mistakes in language use, spelling, or punctuation. However, usually those are the concerns of a proofreader and will be handled in the next chapter.

Whether you write a few sentences, a few paragraphs, or a lengthy report, you need to edit it. You edit your writing by reading it over and looking for passages that might be confusing to another reader, passages that are not really necessary to what you are trying to say, sentences that are out of order, paragraphs that are too long, words that convey gender bias, and so on. You want to bring to your writing all the skills that you have learned in this book so your writing will be the best it can be.

1. Combine short sentences by using appositives (Lesson 3.4) and linking words and phrases (Lesson 4.4).

EXAMPLE

combine 3 sentences { Amir went to technical school. He wanted to be an electronics technician. He was a high school graduate.

combine 2 sentences { Amir was often sick. Amir graduated from the technical school in two years instead of one.

appositive Amir, a high school graduate, went to a technical school

linking word because he wanted to be an electronics technician. *Even though*

linking phrase he was often sick, Amir still graduated from the technical school

linking word in two years instead of one.

Five sentences were edited into two. The linking words and phrases give more meaning to the sentences. Note that ''Amir'' in the fourth sentence was replaced by ''he'' in the second edited sentence, so the name did not need to be repeated.

2. Separate long, run-on sentences into two or more sentences. Be sure to use the correct punctuation.

EXAMPLE

I was so happy when my boss ordered that new word-processing program because I had seen it advertised in a business magazine and I knew it was going to make my work easier once I learned how to use it and I just couldn't wait for it to come in so I could get to work and then I could tell everyone about it.

Edited:

I was so happy when my boss ordered that new word-processing program. I had seen it advertised in a business magazine. I knew it was going to make my work easier once I learned how to use it. I just couldn't wait for it to come in so I could get to work and tell everyone about it.

3. Be sure that subjects and predicates agree (Lesson 3.1) and that verb tenses agree (Lesson 5.1).

EXAMPLE

> Lawanda and Tanya will open a computer store. They sells all kinds of software and hardware. They hire a repairperson who fix any computer. They said their prices are very good.

That paragraph contains past, present, and future tense predicates. The numbers of the subject and predicate do not always agree. Here is the edited version.

> Lawanda and Tanya *opened* a computer store. *They sell* all kinds of software and hardware. Also, they *have hired* a repairperson who *can fix* any computer. Lawanda and Tanya *say* their prices are very good.

The predicate *opened* is past tense because the store is already open. The rest of the predicates are in the present tense. It could also be written in the future tense.

> Lawanda and Tanya *will open* a computer store. They *will sell* all kinds of software and hardware and *will hire* a repairperson who can fix any computer. They say their prices *will be* very good.

Note that *say* is in the present tense because they are talking *now* about the prices they *will charge*.

4. Be sure sentences are in logical order and belong in the paragraph, that is, stick to the point of the paragraph. (Review Lesson 4.2).

5. Look carefully at pronouns to make sure they agree with antecedents (Lesson 1.6). Look at phrases and modifiers to make sure they are not misplaced or dangling (Lesson 3.3).

6. Be sure facts are true and that references are consistent.

EXAMPLE

> Wednesday, January 7
>
> Mr. Mason has called a meeting of all secretaries for 10:00 A.M. tomorrow. It will be in the third-floor conference room. Everyone should be at the meeting Friday afternoon unless excused by a supervisor.

There are two inconsistencies or mistakes.

• The memo is written on Wednesday. If the meeting is "tomorrow," then the last sentence should say "Thursday." Or maybe the reference to "tomorrow" is incorrect.

- The first sentence says the meeting is at 10:00 A.M., but the third sentence says the meeting is in the afternoon. Should "afternoon" be morning, or is the time incorrect?

These are the kinds of things you should look for while editing.

7. Eliminate any gender-biased language (Lesson 5.5).

PRACTICE

1. Circle any mistakes or inconsistencies you see in this paragraph.

The top three salesmen for the month is Anna Alvarez and Todd Wilkins. These people had sales over $10,000 each. Management is proud of them for helping us pass the goal of $100,000. We hope you did as well next week.

Rewrite the paragraph so it is correct and consistent.

_____

_____

_____

_____

_____

_____

_____

_____

_____

_____

_____

2. Edit this paragraph by breaking up run-on sentences, combining too-short sentences, and making any other changes that will make the paragraph better.

Leroy is a bookkeeper. He works for Best Manufacturing. They make all kinds of screws, nuts, and bolts. The bookkeeping department is not very big because it only has four bookkeepers but that is enough because it is a small company. About 75 people work for Best Manufacturing in the shipping department, order department, bookkeeping department, manufacturing department, and design department, and the building is not very big. But it is a nice company to work for and they ship things all over the world.

_____

_____

_____

_____

_____

_____

_____

_____

_____

_____

_____

_____

_____

3. Without thinking about it too much, quickly write a paragraph of six to eight sentences about the first day on a real or imagined job. When you have finished the quick paragraph, read it over carefully. Then rewrite an edited version.

_____

_____

_____

_____

_____

_____

_____

_____

_____

_____

_____

_____

_____

_____

Edited version:

_____

_____

_____

_____

_____

_____

_____

_____

_____

_____

_____

6

Correcting Paragraphs

Proofreader's Marks

∧	caret	Shows where something should be inserted.
⊂		Close up space.
ℐ		Delete one letter or one or more words.
ℒ		Delete and close up space.
#		Space.
/ ⌐		Set in lowercase letter or letters.
≡		Set in capital letters.
∿		Transpose, or reverse, letters or words.
⊙		Period.

EXAMPLE

Dina works for Speedy Temps of america. She usually only works ∅n
Thursdays, Friday AND Saturday⊙ Dina likes d∅oing temporary work
because it gives her a chance to take classes on the other days.

LESSON 6.1

Correct Spelling

Objective   To correctly spell words and to correct misspelled words.

Spelling is a skill that is very important in writing. Misspelled words make writing look careless and unprofessional.

The English language was derived from many different languages, and so it has many strangely spelled words. There are spelling rules to help you, but there are always exceptions to the rules. Words that sound alike are not always spelled with the same letter combinations, and words that are spelled alike are not always pronounced alike.

If you are not sure if you have spelled a word correctly, look up your spelling in a dictionary. If your spelling is not there, you must find the correct spelling.

♦ Spelling Hints

1. Verbs: The rules for spelling the different forms of verbs were given in the first chapter. Go back to pages 16–29 to review them.

2. Reading: In any reading that you do, be aware of the spelling of the words you are reading. If you see a new word, spell it to yourself a few times. Being a good speller is often a matter of knowing when a word looks right or wrong.

3. *ie* and *ei* words: Even good spellers memorize this rhyme to help them remember whether the *i* or the *e* comes first.

    I before E (piece, belief)

    Except after C (receipt, deceit)

    Or when sounded like *ay*

    As in *neighbor* and *weigh*.

Exceptions:

ancient	foreign	leisure	science
conscience	forfeit	neither	seize
either	height	protein	seizure
	heist		weird

4. Sounds like *shun:* The last syllable of *intention* and *fusion* both sound the same—*shun*. Pay special attention to words that end in *-ion,* and learn whether *-ion* has an *s* or a *t* before it.

EXAMPLE

abstention	inflation	ration
association	jurisdiction	relation
commission	lesion	section
coercion	mission	session
detention	omission	tension
dictation	protection	traction
friction	question	vision

5. Sounds like *ur:* The last syllable of *computer, operator,* and *polar* all sound the same—*ur*. Study words that end in the sound *ur* so you know how to spell them. Most of them end in *-er,* so you must be aware of the *-or* and *-ar* exceptions.

   Within words, there are even more variations. All these words have the *-ur* sound; the spelling is usually *-er*.

EXAMPLE

f*ur*ther	resp*ir*ation	m*er*chant
carb*ur*etor	n*ur*se	em*er*gency
stew*ar*d	m*er*ge	s*er*vice
w*or*d	c*ir*cuit	refrig*er*ation
f*ir*st		

6. Sounds like *ay:* These combinations can all sound like *ay: ae, ai, ei, ey,* and *ay*. Observe the words carefully.

EXAMPLE

*ae*rial	camp*ai*gn	arr*ay*
surv*ey*	fr*ei*ght	

7. Sounds like *ee:* These letters and combinations can all sound like *ee: ie, y, e, i, ey,* and *ea*.

EXAMPLE

p*ie*ce   dail*y*   med*i*a   k*ey*   r*ea*d

Frequently Misspelled Words

abridge
access
accommodate
acknowledge
admirable
agreeable
aisle
analyze
annihilate
association
athlete
auxiliary

bazaar
belief
believe
boulevard
built

cancellation
capital
capitol
catalog
ceiling
changeable
chronic
clothes
cloths
colleague
column
condemn
congratulations
counterfeit

defense
deliverance
dependent
descend
dessert
disappoint
disease
disguise
disk (computer)
dissatisfied
duplicate

embarrass
erroneous
exhausted
extraneous

fascinating
forehead
forfeit
formally
formerly
forty

grammar
guarantee
handkerchief
humorous

immediate
immobile
indebtedness
influential
innocence
itemized

judgment

knowledge

league
leisure
license
loose
lose

maintain
maintenance
misspell
monitor

ninety
noticeable

occasional
occur
occurred
occurring
offered
optimist

parenthesis
pastime

permissible
persuade
phenomena
phonic
photocopy
plumbing
pneumonia
preparation
presence
proficiency
psychiatrist
psychology

receipt
recipe
recommend
referred
restaurant
ridiculous

satellite
schedule
separate
sincerely
solemn
stationery
straight
strength
succeed
suede
surgeon

technical
thorough
through
Tuesday

unconscious
unnecessary

vague
volunteer

warranty
Wednesday
word processor
would

yield

PRACTICE

These words are all spelled incorrectly. Give the correct spelling on the line. The first one is done for you.

1. moniter   <u>monitor</u>

2. recieve   _____

3. forinn   _____

4. heighth   _____

5. sectoin   _____

6. murge   _____

7. fraight   _____

8. chronick   _____

9. embaress   _____

10. sincerly   _____

11. dictasion   _____

12. bilt   _____

13. asociation   _____

14. garantey   _____

15. strenth   _____

16. Wensday   _____

17. unsconshus   _____

18. maintenence   _____

19. conferrence   _____

20. teknishun   _____

21. sterilise   _____

22. salarys   _____

23. prepard   _____

24. typeing   _____

25. skiming   _____

Troublesome Words

Objective   To be aware of words that cause trouble in spelling and/or use.

♦ Homonyms

Homonyms are words that sound the same or almost the same but are spelled differently and have different meanings. Therefore, you have to be careful to use the correct word. Here are some of the more common homonyms.

Common Homonyms

accept-except	fair-fare	pain-pane
affect-effect	find-fined	pair-pare-pear
air-heir	for-four	peace-piece
aisle-isle-I'll	grate-great	plain-plane
allowed-aloud	guessed-guest	principal-principle
altar-alter	hall-haul	profit-prophet
assistance-assistants	heal-heel	rain-reign-rein
band-banned	hear-here	read-reed
bare-bear	heard-herd	real-reel
berry-bury	higher-hire	right-rite-write
blew-blue	hole-whole	road-rode-rowed
boar-bore	hour-our	role-roll
born-borne	in-inn	root-route
brake-break	instance-instants	sail-sale
capital-capitol	it's-its	scene-seen
carat-caret-carrot	know-no	sea-see
cell-sell	lessen-lesson	sew-so-sow
cent-scent-sent	loan-lone	some-sum
cite-sight-site	mail-male	stake-steak
coarse-course	main-mane	stair-stare
council-counsel	meat-meet	stationary-stationery
councillor-counselor	none-nun	steal-steel
dual-duel	one-won	straight-strait
earn-urn	pail-pale	suite-sweet
faint-feint		threw-through

their-there-they're	wait-weight	which-witch
to-too-two	ware-wear-where	who's-whose
vain-vein-vane	weak-week	wood-would
waist-waste	weather-whether	your-you're

♦ Contractions

A *contraction* is a word that has been formed from two words by the omission of some letters. An apostrophe shows where the letters were omitted. The contractions below are in the homonym list with the word they sound like. If you are not sure which word to use, change the contraction back to its two-word form. If that does not make sense in the sentence, use the other word.

it's-its _____ a long letter.
It's (It is) a long letter.

you're-your _____ going to get a raise.
You're (You are) going to get a raise.

they're-their _____ on vacation.
They're (They are) on vacation.

who's-whose _____ in charge of this project?
Who's (Who is) in charge of this project?

♦ Prepositions

Refer back to Lesson 1.17 for the correct use of *beside* and *besides, in* and *into, between* and *among,* and *like* and *as.*

♦ Adverbs

Refer back to Lesson 1.15 for the correct use of *well,* as opposed to *good.*

very and *real*—*very* is an adverb.
real is an adjective meaning "not fake."

EXAMPLE

A computer repairperson has to be *very* good with small parts. (*not* real good; *very* modifies the adjective *good*)

surely and *sure*—*surely* is an adverb meaning "certainly."
sure is an adjective meaning "to be certain."

EXAMPLE

Susan is *surely* a good computer programmer. (not *sure*)
Are you *sure* of the meeting time?

almost and *most—almost* is an adverb meaning ''nearly, or just about.''

most can be an adverb or an adjective meaning ''the greatest.''

EXAMPLE

Mr. Hanson *almost* missed his plane.
André is our *most* successful salesperson. (adverb)
Janine has the *most* experience with that program. (adjective)

then and *than—then* is an adverb meaning ''at that time.''
than is a conjunction used for comparison.

EXAMPLE

Please, type this letter and *then* mail it.
This copier is much faster *than* the old one.

The meaning of some verbs gets confused. Here are some of the more common verb problems.

lie and *lay—lie* refers to a person or thing *lying* down.
The past tense of *lie* is *lay*.

EXAMPLE

The paper *lies* on the desk.
Yesterday, the paper *lay* on the desk.

—*lay* (a verb in the present tense) refers to something being put down.
The past tense of lay is *laid*.

EXAMPLE

He *lays* the paper on the desk.
Yesterday, he *laid* the paper on the desk.

Lie and *lay* cannot be interchanged. *Lie* never has an object. *Lay* always has an object.

sit and *set*—*sit* refers to taking a seat. The past tense of *sit* is *sat*. Like *lie, sit* never has an object.

EXAMPLE

Please *sit* in that chair.
I *sat* in this chair before.

—*set* refers to putting something somewhere. The past tense of *set* is *set*. Like *lay, set* always has an object.

EXAMPLE

He *set* the printer on the table.
Last week, I *set* the printer on the shelf.

rise and *raise*—*rise* refers to getting up or going up. It never has an object.

EXAMPLE

Profits *rise* when sales are up.

—*raise* refers to something going up. It may have an object.

EXAMPLE

The jack *raised* the front of the car.
The curtain *was raised* to reveal the display.

teach and *learn*—*teach* refers to instructing someone.

EXAMPLE

I *will teach* you how to boot up the computer.
(NOT I will learn you how to boot up the computer.)

—*learn* refers to obtaining knowledge.

EXAMPLE

Fran *is learning* to use the computer.

leave and *let*—*leave* refers to departing from a place or allowing to remain.

EXAMPLE

I will *leave* the office at 4:30.
Did you *leave* your briefcase here?

—*let* refers to permitting.

EXAMPLE

Mr. Frank is going to *let* me try the new computer.
(NOT *leave* me try the new computer.)

may and *can*—*may* refers to permission.

EXAMPLE

May I go to lunch early today? (This means "Am I permitted?"
Many people would say "Can I go," but that is not correct.)

—*can* refers to ability.

EXAMPLE

Can you hear the phone from there? (This means "*Are you able* to
hear?")

PRACTICE

Underline the correct word to complete the sentence. The first one is done
for you.

1. Be sure the paper is (straight, strait) in the printer.
2. Alicia and Dwayne shared the job (between, among) them.
3. She is a (real, very) fine typist.
4. When I went to donate blood, I was told to (lie, lay) on a cot.
5. My supervisor was (formerly, formally) my co-worker.
6. The office is (highering, hiring) a consultant to (learn, teach) us how to use the new program.
7. (Can, May) that copier make color copies?
8. (Their, They're) not going to like all these changes.
9. It is easier to get parts for (some, sum) cars than others.
10. Connor was (surely, sure) that he had placed the order in time.
11. The bank teller could probably find out the balance in (your, you're) checking account.
12. Will your boss (let, leave) you (let, leave) early tomorrow?
13. Melanie is going to take a (course, coarse) in data processing so she can look for a better job.
14. Right now, airfares are cheaper (then, than) train fares.
15. (Besides, Beside) plumbing, Gigi is also interested in carpentry.

16. Frankie just received his (fourth, forth) job offer.

17. The waiter (sat, set) the menu down in front of me.

18. Laser printers give you copies that do not look (as, like) copies.

19. When our company moved, we had to order new (stationery, stationary).

20. Tawanna has (almost, most) beaten Saul's record for new sales contracts.

21. (Who's, Whose) advice is more valuable—mine or your doctor's?

22. Please (lie, lay) that file on Kelly's desk.

23. I (guest, guessed) that the verdict would be ''not guilty.''

24. That computer requires that the disk be put (in, into) the drive before the computer is turned on.

25. Ms. Flori said I (may, can) go to the conference with you.

LESSON 6.3

Correct Capitalization

Objective   To correctly capitalize words.

Words that begin with capital letters are:

1. The first word in any sentence.

2. Proper nouns (people, places, days of the week, months, brand names, holidays, special events, etc.).

3. Proper adjectives (adjectives that are made from proper nouns).

4. The first, last, and every main word in a title (that excludes prepositions, conjunctions, and articles).

5. The pronoun I.

6. Titles of respect or position.

EXAMPLE

1. Postage for the first ounce of first-class mail costs $0.29. The second ounce costs $0.23.

2. Jake is flying to New York with Nadia.

   The Summer Olympic Games were held in Barcelona, Spain, in 1992.

   I bet a lot of Kleenex are sold in January.

   People travel the most on the Thanksgiving weekend.

   The White House is the residence of U.S. presidents.

3. Many tourists travel to American cities.

   I work for a firm that imports Swiss chocolates.

4. The longest book I ever read was *Gone with the Wind*.

   Monty finds a lot of good information in *Computer Weekly*.

   I enjoyed watching the television special "The Life and Times of Andrew Carnegie."

5. May I get you something?

6. The chairman of the board of this company is Mrs. Janice Williams.

   Let me introduce Chairman Williams.

   This plane is being flown by Captain Diaz.

   A drastic change in the treatment of polio was made by Sister Elizabeth Kenny.

Making corrections:

1. If a capital letter should be a lowercase letter, draw a diagonal line through it.

   N̸orthern route

   If a group of capital letters should be lowercase, draw a diagonal line attached to a horizontal line.

   C̸OMPUTER monitor

2. If a lowercase letter should be a capital letter, draw three horizontal lines under it.

   Los angeles, California

   ibm computer

PRACTICE

Mark the letters that should be capitals. The first one is done for you.

1. I work in the seagram's building on park avenue.

2. our fiscal year begins on july 1.

3. the first typewriter was manufactured by e. remington and sons.

4. sid is an assistant to an occupational therapist at saint joseph's hospital.

5. the computer came with a book titled *getting to know your computer*.

6. new year's day is a national holiday in the united states.

7. mrs. boudreau comes to collect the rent on the first thursday of the month.

8. do you prefer apple, ibm, or hewlitt-packard computers?

9. the contributions of workers are recognized on labor day, the first monday in september in the united states and canada.

10. brian clarkson replaced president stein as head of our firm.

Mark the letters that should be lowercase. The first one is done for you.

11. *Roger And Me* is an interesting Documentary about working people.
12. Both Men and Women have to take exams for Civil Service jobs.
13. The Bank is open until 8:00 P.M. on Thursday and FRIDAY evenings.
14. My mother went to Night School to learn Secretarial skills.
15. When Roxy becomes a Nurse's Aide, She is moving to the City of Philadelphia.

LESSON 6.4

Correct Punctuation

Objective   To insert correct punctuation and to remove incorrect or unnecessary punctuation.

As you learned in Lesson 3.2, there are two kinds of punctuation: end punctuation (the marks that are made at the end of a sentence or after an interjection) and internal punctuation (the marks that are made within a sentence).

End Punctuation

period .
exclamation point !
question mark ?

A *period* goes at the end of declarative and imperative sentences (for review, see Lesson 2.2).

EXAMPLE

This is a computer. (declarative)
Move that computer. (imperative)

An *exclamation point* goes at the end of an exclamatory sentence (for review, see Lesson 2.2) or after an interjection (for review, see Lesson 1.19).

EXAMPLE

That was great! (exclamatory)
Hurray! (interjection)

A *question mark* goes at the end of an interrogative sentence (for review, see Lesson 2.2) or after an interrogative pronoun or adverb.

EXAMPLE

Is she the new teller?
Where did you put that file?
Whom would you like to see?
What?
Who?

Internal Punctuation

Comma ,
Semicolon ;
Colon :
Hyphen -
Dash —
Parentheses ( )
Quotation marks " "
Period . (with abbreviations)

A *comma* is used to separate words, numbers, or parts of a sentence (for review, see Lessons 3.2, 3.4, and 3.5).

EXAMPLE

"Steve, when you finish typing that letter, I would like you to copy, collate, and mail it," Ms. Barker said.

Crystal, my doctor's medical assistant, graduated from the same school that I did, but she was two years before me.

On May 12, 1980, the company moved to Reno, Nevada.

A *semicolon* separates the clauses of a compound sentence when a conjunction is not used (for review, see Lesson 3.2).

EXAMPLE

The appointment for the blood test is tomorrow; you should not eat or drink anything but water for 12 hours before the test.

A *colon* indicates a list or series (for review, see Lesson 3.2).

EXAMPLE

You can have your flier copied on seven colors of paper: white, yellow, mint, sky blue, lavender, gold, and ivory.

A *hyphen* joins the parts of a compound word and goes at the end of a line of type when a word must be broken.

EXAMPLE

During the summer, our company works four 10-hour days.

A *dash* takes the place of a comma or semicolon when a stronger break is needed or to avoid confusion with other commas.

EXAMPLE

Housing sales increased—increased very sharply—when mortgage rates dropped.

Parentheses separate unnecessary material from the rest of a sentence. They are stronger than commas, and they always appear in pairs.

EXAMPLE

Wanda's secretarial skills (typing, filing, organizing, and so on) get better each year.

Quotation marks show the actual words of a speaker (for review, see Lesson 3.5). They always appear in pairs.

EXAMPLE

The caller said, ''This is Tony Andrews. May I speak to the manager?''

A *period* shows the end of an abbreviation.

EXAMPLE

Mr. John E. Montezi from U.S. Cottons, Inc., is on the phone.

Making corrections:

Insert a comma or semicolon—
Insert quotation marks—
Insert a period—⊙
Insert a colon—⊙
Insert parentheses—( )
Insert a hyphen— =
Insert a dash—
Insert on exclamation point— !
Insert a question mark— ?

EXAMPLE

Mandy, a dental assistant, will not be at work today. Do you know why? She (and her sister) are attending a conference to view new equipment, new cleaning tools, new toothpaste, new head rests, and so on. Her employer, Dr. Galardi, paid the conference fee. When she told me, I said, ''Wow! That was nice of him.''

PRACTICE

The following sentences have incorrect punctuation. Circle the mistakes, then rewrite each sentence with correct punctuation. The first one is done for you.

1. When the supplier calls ;   please let me know ?
    When the supplier calls, please let me know.
    _____

2. Jamal: you should be in court July 12, at 10 in the morning!

    _____

    _____

3. Mr, Whitfield called and said; You have the job,

    _____

    _____

4. The meeting in Chicago; Illinois. is taking place on Monday Tuesday
    and Wednesday?

    _____

    _____

5. My partner (Andy Maciel) gave Mrs: Quinn the estimate—to fix her
    bumper!

    _____

    _____

6. Read the following paragraph. Look for places that need punctuation,
    and mark the correction.

    At Peoples Bank in Bridgeport Connecticut employees view a video

    showing an angry customer talking to a teller Then the employees discuss

    what might have occurred in the customer's day before the visit to the bank

    You cannot control events in your customer's day or your customer's

    feelings about the day says Carole Callahan manager of management

    development Employees learn self-management techniques Instead of

    blaming themselves when faced with an angry customer employees learn to

    remain calm to empathize and to ask themselves what they can do to

    improve the situation Callahan says

LESSON 6.5

Proofreading

Objective   To proofread typewritten copy.

A **proofreader** is someone who reads typed copy and looks for mistakes and for things that have been left out.

The proofreader finds mistakes, marks them to be deleted (taken out), and writes in the correct punctuation, word, spelling, and so on.

The proofreader finds places where letters, words, punctuation, and so on have been left out and marks where the material should be added.

If there is room in the typed copy, the correction or addition is marked where it should be.

If there is no room, the change is marked in the margin right next to the line where it should go. If there is more than one correction in the same line, they are written in the margin, in order from left to right, with a slanted line / between them.

The proofreader's marks are shown before Lesson 6.1.

EXAMPLE

A dental assistant is persn who works at a dentist's side. Thne assistant helps

the dentist by passing instruments, preparing fillings,and make the patient /ing

comfortable/ a dental usually works monday through friday. /assistant

PRACTICE

Proofread each sentence and correct any errors. The first one is done for you.

1. when a car is damaged in an accident it taken to an auto-body shop it

    repairs

2. A computer only work on the Data it is gven; from a floppy disk or from

    a hard drive?

3. A Bank offers such services as saving lending andd checking

4. if someone wants to be a nurse's aide that person should haave an interest in Medicine THE person shuld also, be able to follow orders exactly and like taking care people.

5. A legal stenographer sits in a courtroom everyday. he or she listens to every word tht is said by witnesses; lawyers; and the judge and records in on special typewriter

7

Exercises in Career Writing

Business Letters

Objective   To learn and use the correct form for a business letter.

A *business letter* is usually written in formal language, as opposed to the informal language of a personal letter. It can be written to request a job, to gain information about a product or company, to complain about service, and so on. A business letter is written in a certain form.

1. | return address |

2. | date |

3. | inside address |

4. | greeting *saludo verbo comunicato* |

5. | body of letter |

6. | closing |

7. | signature |

8. | typed name |

The letter form on page 133 shows items 1, 2, 6, 7, and 8 indented and aligned under one another. Items 3, 4, and 5 are aligned at the left margin. The same items appear in the following form, but all the items align at the left margin.

1. | return address |

2. | date |

3. | inside address |

4. | greeting |

5.
| body of letter |

6. | closing |

7. | signature |

8. | typed name |

1. return address   street address (or box number) city, state, and ZIP code of writer

2. date   month, day, and year when letter is being written (outside of United States, it is day, month, year)

3. inside address   the name (with any titles) and complete address of person or company receiving letter

(**Note:** No abbreviations are used unless they are part of a business name; for example, Inc.)

4. greeting   Dear _____ with person's last name if letter is going to specific person; otherwise, Dear Sir, Dear Madam, Dear Sir or Madam, or Gentlemen or Ladies. Always followed by a *colon*.

5. body of letter   First sentence is reason for letter; following sentences explain and support reason; last sentence closes letter, makes final request or statement, and so on. Language should be business-like. Message should be clear and simple (not a lot of extra words).

6. closing   Sincerely, Sincerely yours, or Yours truly are acceptable closings (always followed by comma).

7. signature   first and last name of writer of letter—middle initial may be included (no nickname)

8. typed name (and title, if any)   given to avoid misreading of written name

EXAMPLE

Answering a job ad:

---

421 North Street
Yonkers, New York 10703

May 22, 1993

Ms. Celine Murphy
    Personnel Director
Newtone Computers, Inc.
379 First Street
Providence, Rhode Island 02905

Dear Ms. Murphy:

I am writing to answer your ad for a secretary in the May 19 *Yonkers Herald*.

I graduated from secretarial school on May 10, 1993, and would like to be considered for a job with your company. I have excellent word-processing skills and am familiar with Macintosh and IBM computers.

I have enclosed my résumé, which details my education and other job experience, and can supply references at your request. I will call you Tuesday morning to set a time for an appointment. I look forward to speaking with you.

Sincerely,

Jordan Murdock

Jordan Murdock

If you are writing on letterhead stationery, then the return address is omitted.

EXAMPLE

Requesting a catalog:

Escobar Industries
P.O. Box 9308
4126 Mill Drive
Little Falls, Utah 00000

September 16, 1993

Best Paper Products
352 Industrial Drive
Middletown, Michigan 00000

Dear Sir or Madam:

I am writing to request a catalog of your products. I am most interested in types of computer paper and any labels, forms, and so on, that can be used on a computer printer.

Thank you for your attention.

Yours truly,

Anita Renoni

Anita Renoni
Purchasing Coordinator

PRACTICE

1. Use your own name and address and today's date. Write a letter to Super Computer Products, 5241 Main Street, Oldville, New York 11111. You

ordered a computer printer (Model X237A), but they sent the wrong one (Model X239A). The letter should tell them about the mistake they made and ask for a correction.

_____

_____

_____

_____

_____

_____

_____

_____

_____

_____

_____

_____

_____

_____

_____

_____

2. Use your own name and address and today's date. Answer the following ad, which you saw in the *Providence Journal* on July 3, 1993.

General Office: Will perform general clerical duties such as typing, filing, compiling reports, and answering phones. Computer experience necessary. Must be detail oriented and willing to learn. Send résumé to: Box M–2467 Journal Building, 823 Fountain Street, Providence, RI 02900.

_____

_____

_____

_____

_____

_____

_____

_____

_____

_____

_____

_____

_____

_____

_____

_____

_____

LESSON 7.2

Memos

Objective   To write a clear, informative memo.

Memo is short for *memorandum*. A memo is a short note or reminder circulated to one or more people.

Sometimes a memo is written on a form. Sometimes you write your own memo. It usually looks like this:

TO:	Copy Department Staff
FROM:	Mitchell Conlon, Supervisor
DATE:	March 5, 1993
RE: (or TOPIC)	Recycling paper

This is just to remind you of the company's paper-recycling policies. White paper must be separated from colored. No magazines or newspapers should be put in with computer paper and stationery. Be sure no trash ends up in the recycling bins.
You cooperation is appreciated.

A memo could also look like this:

From the desk

of

Lucille Kupeck

TO: Vanda Chora

DATE: October 6, Wednesday

SUBJECT: Lunch

Vanda, I just want to remind you of our lunch date on Friday. See you at the Blue Diner at 12:30.

A memo is short. The information is specific.

PRACTICE

1. Write a memo to your department about the office picnic on September 3 in River Park. The company is supplying hot dogs, hamburgers, drinks, cups, and plates. The rest (salads and desserts) is potluck (the people bring them). Tell the people what to bring and what to do if it rains.

_____

_____

_____

_____

_____

_____

_____

_____

_____

2. Write a memo to your boss reminding her of the Friday morning meeting. Tell her where and when and the reason for the meeting.

_____

_____

_____

_____

_____

_____

_____

_____

_____

3. You are a dental secretary. Write a memo to a patient reminding him or her of the scheduled checkup. Make up the name, date, and time.

_____

_____

_____

_____

_____

_____

_____

_____

_____

4. You are a secretary in the mortgage department of a bank. Write a memo to the personnel department requesting that they line up a temporary bookkeeper for the month of April. Make up whatever information you think is necessary.

_____

_____

_____

_____

_____

_____

_____

_____

_____

LESSON 7.3

Invitations, Formal and Informal

Objective   To write a clear and complete invitation.

An *invitation* is a note inviting one or more people to an event. It may be formal or informal. It may be printed or handwritten.
An invitation must state:

1. The name of the sender of the invitation.
2. The event.
3. The date and time of the event.
4. The place.
5. Whether or not a reply is requested.

Formal invitations are written in third person; they are usually printed, but may be handwritten.

> Dr. Philip R. Dubois
>
> cordially invites
>
> you and your family
>
> to join him and his staff
>
> to celebrate the opening
>
> of
>
> the new Family Medicine Center
>
> Sunday, February 6, 1993
>
> 1:00 to 4:00 P.M.
>
> 49 Center Street
>
> Dalesville, New York

In the given invitation, "cordially invites" could be replaced with words like "requests the pleasure of the company of" or "requests the honor of your presence at." The wording often depends on the formality of the occasion.

Informal invitations are usually handwritten; they may be a note or a purchased invitation with blank spaces for the information.

A Note:

> Dear Taylor,
>
>   I'm giving a dinner party to celebrate Jack's promotion to head teller. It will be on Friday night, October 15, at 7:00, at our home, 61 Maple Drive. Hope you can make it.
>
>   Sincerely,
>   Marcia Burton
>
> RSVP   555-9690 by October 12

A Card:

> A party for   Jack Burton
>
> In honor of   promotion to head teller
>
> Given by   Marcia Burton
>
> Date   Friday, October 15
>
> Time   7:00 P.M.
>
> Place   61 Maple Drive
>
> RSVP   555-9690 by October 12

Note that the invitation to the Family Medicine Center did not have RSVP (which is French for "answer please"). The party is more of an open house, and it does not matter how many people come. However, for a dinner party, one needs to know how many people to cook for.

Some invitations end with "Regrets only." That means you have to call the host or hostess only if you are *not going* to the party. The host or hostess assumes everyone is coming unless he or she hears otherwise.

PRACTICE

1. Simmons Real Estate is having coffee hour, 10–11:30 A.M., on August 17, 1993, to celebrate their first year in business. Write a formal invitation.

2. Write a note to a co-worker asking him or her to attend a trade show on computers and computer software.

3. Frank Jackson is being honored at a dinner given for the top salesperson of the month of June. The dinner is being given by the St. Louis Office Supplies Company at the company headquarters. You fill in the card below, making up the date and so on.

A dinner for   _____

on the occasion of   _____

_____

Given by   _____

on   _____

at   _____

_____

RSVP

LESSON 7.4

Filling Out Forms

Objective   To fill out forms completely and accurately.

In one of the invitation forms in Lesson 7.3, you filled in blanks to supply the necessary information. There are many other times when you will be filling out forms—applying to a school, applying for a job, completing income tax forms, and so on.

The information on these forms must be accurate (true, as far as you know), as complete as you can make it, neat, and easy to read (usually hand-printed or typed rather than written).

You must read the form's directions carefully. Does the last name go first or the first name? Should you print? Must you fill in all the blanks? And so on.

A form can be as simple as one to subscribe to a magazine or as complicated as one to apply for a line of credit.

EXAMPLE

The following form is one that allows a university to receive automatic monthly tuition payments from a person's checking account. If you were taking courses at a university, you might use this kind of form so you would not have to pay all the tuition at once and so you would not have to write out a check each month.

The left side of the form is completed. Nothing is written in the right side because it says "FOR OFFICE USE ONLY."

Authorization for Delay Pay Plan:

FOR OFFICE USE ONLY

STUDENT'S LAST NAME, FIRST NAME, MIDDLE INITIAL

| M | A | R | C | H | O | N | | B | R | I | T | T | A | N | Y | | L | | | |

STUDENT'S ID NUMBER

| 1 | 2 | 3 | 4 | 5 | 6 |
49   54

STUDENT'S U.S. SOCIAL SECURITY NUMBER

| 1 | 1 | 1 | | 2 | 2 | | 3 | 3 | 3 | 3 |
40   48

Depository ANY NATIONAL BANK   Bank's tel. no. 111-555-9999

Address 67 EIGHTH STREET   YOURTOWN   NJ   02000
              street   city   state   zip code

Account number   987654321

I (we) hereby authorize the University to initiate preauthorized electronic fund transfers from my (our) checking account indicated above, and I (we) authorize the depository named above to debit the transfers to that account. The authorization is to remain in effect until the University and the depository have received written notification from me (or either of us) of its termination and have had reasonable opportunity to act on it.

Signature _Brittany L. Marchon_   7/12/94
         person authorized to sign checks on this account   date

Student's name BRITTANY L. MARCHON   7/12/94
                                    date

Parent's signature _Andrew C. Marchon_   7/12/94
                                    date

ADD
PRE

| 6 | | 2 | 7 | | 0 | 2 |
1   2   3   79   80

Batch # _____

Type of contract:
12-month plan
10-month plan
Fall-only plan
Spring-only plan

4   TRANSIT ROUTING NO.   11   12
                                    RET. CK.

13   BANK ACCOUNT NUMBER TO BE CHARGED   29
         (LEFT JUSTIFIED, TRAILING BLANKS)

30   AMOUNT PER MONTH   49

55   ACCOUNT HOLDER'S LAST NAME, FIRST NAME   76

Note that the writing is neat and readable. Note that all the blanks on the left side are filled in.

PRACTICE

Fill in each form with your own information. Make up any information that you cannot get from your own background. If a form asks for information that does not apply to you (for example, a spouse's occupation, but you are single) (write N/A for "does not apply"). If a form requires numbers that do not apply to you, you can either put zeros (00.00) or a dash (—) in that spot.

Read any directions carefully.

1. Magazine subscription

JOB
MAGAZINE

☐ Please enter my one-year subscription
(9 issues) at the low basic rate of $18.
And be sure to send my commemorative
stoneware mug when my payment is received.

☐ Payment of $18 is enclosed.
☐ Bill me.

Name _____

Address _____

City, State, Zip _____

Telephone Number _____

JOB Magazine • P.O. Box 0 • Marion, Ohio 43300

2. Insurance information request

YES!

*I'm interested in learning
more about how Best Life
can help me plan for the
future.*

*Please enclose this card with
your premium payment.*

Mail to:
**Best Life Insurance Co.
100 Best Boulevard
New York, NY 10000**

Please contact me. I'm especially interested in:

☐ Providing for my family's
financial future

☐ Planning for retirement

☐ Funding my child's college
education

☐ Saving for the future with
mutual funds and annuities

☐ Health insurance or
disability insurance

☐ Insurance for my home
or car

☐ A dynamic career
opportunity as an
Account Representative

Name _____

Street Address _____

City _____ State _____ Zip _____

Telephone (___)_____ Best Time to Call _____

Policy Number _____ Sales Office/Agy _____

3.   Course registration

**Enrollment Form
Fall 1993**

You can enroll by phone
with Visa or Mastercard
Call 401–555–3452

or return to:
Learning Community
Alumnae Hall
Providence, RI 02900

(Please print)

Name _____
LAST, FIRST, MIDDLE

Address _____
STREET   APARTMENT NO.

_____ Date _____
CITY, STATE   ZIP

Occupation _____ Birthdate _____
MONTH/YEAR

Employer _____

Daytime Telephone _____ Home Telephone _____
AREA CODE, NUMBER, EXT.   AREA CODE, NUMBER

Have you been enrolled in a Learning Community Course before?   ☐ Yes   ☐ No

---

Course Selection

	COURSE NUMBER	COURSE TITLE	TUITION
1.	__ – __ __ __ – __	_____	$_____
2.	__ – __ __ __ – __	_____	$_____
3.	__ – __ __ __ – __	_____	$_____
4.	__ – __ __ __ – __	_____	$_____
5.	__ – __ __ __ – __	_____	$_____

LC Membership

Joining the Learning Community
is optional. Individual membership
benefits include:

• With one course at full tuition, 50%
  discount off most additional courses
  of equal or lower tuition.

• Access to libraries.

• Discounts on athletic facilities use.

• Eligibility for auditing or enrolling
  in regular university courses.

Registration Fee:
(per person) $ **5.00**

Subtotal: $_____

Optional
LC individual
Membership Fee:
($30 a semester) $_____

**LC Individual
Member Discount:**
(with one course at full
tuition, take 50% off other
courses of equal or lower
tuitions, except where noted
in course description)   – $_____

Total: $_____

*Note: Membership and enrollment in the
Learning Community is conditional and requires
compliance with all University rules and regulations.
Persons who have been trespassed or otherwise
excluded from the University campus are not eligible
for membership and enrollment.*

Method of Payment:

I.   ☐ Check _____
        BANK   CHECK NO.
     ☐ Money Order *(payable to Learning Community)*

II. ☐ Mastercard   ☐ Visa

     Exp. Date _____

     Card No. _____

     Signature _____

FOR OFFICE USE ONLY

☐ 100 _____   ☐ 200 _____
☐ 101 _____   ☐ 201 _____
☐ 102 _____   ☐ 202 _____
☐ 103 _____   ☐ 203 _____

4.   Credit card application

CREDIT CARD APPLICATION

Credit Line Requested: _____ $250 _____ $500 _____ $750

| Name: | Social Security No.: | Date of Birth: |

| Home Address/No. Street: | City/Town: | State: | Zip: | Phone: ( ) |

| Employed by: | Trade name if self-employed: |

Type of business:

| Address: | How long here: |

| Position: | Bus. Phone: ( ) |

Monthly Rent or Mortgage:

Credit Information: Please show all charge accounts, installment contracts, education loans, or any other obligations for which you are liable or which you are authorized to use.   (Use separate sheet if necessary.)

BANK/FINANCE CO./CREDIT UNION	ORIGINAL AMOUNT/ CREDIT LINE	UNPAID BALANCE	MONTHLY PAYMENT
1.	$	$	$
2.	$	$	$
3.	$	$	$
4.	$	$	$

Gross Monthly Income $: _____   Other Income $: _____   Source: _____

Income from alimony, child support or separate maintenance need not be revealed if you choose not to rely on it to repay this obligation.

AUTO TELLER 24-BANKING

Your card can be encoded with a six-digit personal identification number (PIN) to activate Auto Teller automated teller machines so that you may obtain a cash advance against your savings account. So that we may properly encode your card, please select the six digits of your choice. (This six-digit number will be known only to you and the bank.)

☐ ☐ ☐ ☐ ☐ ☐

_____
Savings Account Number

_____   _____
Account Owner's Signature   Date

PLEASE READ AND SIGN:

All information on this application is true and complete. Bank is authorized to obtain further credit information from any source. Applicant requests issuance of a card and agrees to be bound by the terms and conditions of the Credit Card Agreement received with the card and the Write-A-Loan checks. Applicant agrees that the terms of the section of the Credit Card Agreement titled "Auto Teller Services" shall apply to each of the accounts listed on this application.

_____   _____
Applicant Signature   Date

Please do not send payment of the annual membership fee. If your application is approved you will be billed when your account is opened and on the date your account is renewed each year thereafter.

Bank use Only	Approved	Number	SV $ Line	Date

5. Catalog order form

Daytime Phone (_____) _____

01000

PLEASE
PLACE PEEL-OFF
LABEL HERE

THIS SPACE FOR ADDRESS CORRECTION OR USE IF LABEL IS MISSING

☐ Mr.
☐ Mrs.
☐ Miss

PLEASE USE SAME NAME AND ADDRESS FOR ALL ORDERS FROM YOUR HOUSEHOLD

Address   Apt.

City   State   Zip

Item Number	How Many?	Item and Personalization (PLEASE PRINT PLAINLY)	Page No.	✔	Price Each	Total Price
		MINIMUM MERCHANDISE ORDER $5.00				

PLEASE ADD FOR SHIPPING & HANDLING	
Up to $7.00 .... Add $1.95	
$ 7.01 to $13.00 .... Add $2.95	
$13.01 to $20.00 .... Add $3.95	
$20.01 to $35.00 .... Add $4.95	
$35.01 to $50.00 .... Add $5.95	
Over $50.00 .... Add $6.95	

Each package sent to a separate address requires separate postage.

Please note that this company does not charge extra for insurance.

EVERY ITEM GUARANTEED!

Total for Merchandise	
Shipping and Handling	
"INSURANCE"	FREE
Wisconsin Residents Only: Add 5% Sales Tax to Total Merchandise & Shipping Costs	
Total Amount Enclosed	

6.   Job application form

AMERICAN INDUSTRIES, INC. — APPLICATION FOR EMPLOYMENT

LAST NAME	FIRST	MIDDLE	SOCIAL SECURITY NO.	
PRESENT ADDRESS			TELEPHONE	
CITY	STATE	ZIP	HEIGHT	WEIGHT
PERMANENT ADDRESS			TELEPHONE	
CITY	STATE	ZIP	U.S. CITIZEN	
REFERRED BY:				
RELATIVE EMPLOYED BY COMPANY? NAME/DEPT.				

IN EMERGENCY: NAME/ADDRESS	TELEPHONE
PERSONAL PHYSICIAN: NAME/ADDRESS	TELEPHONE

EDUCATION

ELEMENTARY SCHOOL - NAME/LOCATION	YEARS ATTENDED	DATE GRADUATED
HIGH SCHOOL - NAME/LOCATION	YEARS ATTENDED	GRADUATED? ☐ YES ☐ NO WHEN
	MAJOR SUBJECT AREA	
COLLEGE/TECHNICAL	YEARS ATTENDED	DATE GRADUATED
	MAJOR	DEGREE RECEIVED
COLLEGE/TECHNICAL	YEARS ATTENDED	DATE GRADUATED
	MAJOR	DEGREE RECEIVED
MEMBER PROFESSIONAL ORGANIZATION	REGISTRATION NUMBER	
MEMBER PROFESSIONAL ORGANIZATION	REGISTRATION NUMBER	
SUBJECTS OF SPECIAL STUDY/RESEARCH		
BUSINESS MACHINES YOU CAN OPERATE		

(Vertical labels in left margin of EDUCATION section: MIDDLE, FIRST, LAST NAME)

LESSON 7.5

Taking Messages

Objective   To take a complete and clear message.

Whether at work or at home, taking a message for someone can be a great responsibility. Most offices have forms like the following to make message taking easier.

The person leaving the message may be on the telephone or may be talking to you directly. You should get the same information either way. Be sure names are spelled correctly and phone numbers are correct.

EXAMPLE

To _Jean Tassoni_
Date _9/8/93_ ___ Time _9:30_ ___ ☑AM ☐PM

WHILE YOU WERE OUT

Mr. _Decker_

of _____

Phone _(123)_ _555-1111_ _x999_
     Area Code   Number   Extension

TELEPHONED	✓	PLEASE CALL	✓
CALLED TO SEE YOU		WILL CALL AGAIN	
WANTS TO SEE YOU		URGENT	
	RETURNED YOUR CALL		

Message _____
_____
_____
_____
_____
_____
_____
                              Jared
                              Operator

Look at the form. Why does the third line just have an M_____? It tells you that the caller's name goes there, and it is the first letter of Mr., Mrs., Ms., and Miss.

The middle part of the form is a check-off list. It makes one part of the message taking easier.

The bottom part gives you room to write any particular message.

PRACTICE

1. Take a message on form 1: Ms. Alix Pearson from Coffee Service, Inc., called to set up the time for the next delivery. She left her number as 345-555-0606. That is her direct line. Make up any other information you need.

Form I

```
To _____
                                               ☐ AM
Date _____ Time _____             ☐ PM

WHILE YOU WERE OUT

M _____

of _____

Phone ( _____ ) _____
          Area Code        Number        Extension

┌─────────────────────┬──┬──────────────────┬──┐
│ TELEPHONED          │  │ PLEASE CALL      │  │
├─────────────────────┼──┼──────────────────┼──┤
│ CALLED TO SEE YOU   │  │ WILL CALL AGAIN  │  │
├─────────────────────┼──┼──────────────────┼──┤
│ WANTS TO SEE YOU    │  │ URGENT           │  │
└─────────────────────┴──┴──────────────────┴──┘
         │ RETURNED YOUR CALL │  │

Message _____

_____

_____

_____

_____

_____

_____

_____
                              Operator
```

2. Take a message on form 2: Jason Bedard's mother called to remind him of his father's birthday on Friday. Make up any other information you can.

Form 2

To _____	
Date _____ Time _____	☐ AM ☐ PM

WHILE YOU WERE OUT

M _____

of _____

Phone (_____) _____

           Area Code   Number   Extension

TELEPHONED		PLEASE CALL	
CALLED TO SEE YOU		WILL CALL AGAIN	
WANTS TO SEE YOU		URGENT	
	RETURNED YOUR CALL		

Message _____

_____

_____

_____

_____

_____

_____

                                                Operator

3. Write out a message to your boss from Max Literhood, his insurance agent. He has some new information for the boss about the insurance of the office building and its contents. He wants the boss to call him before Thursday (this is Monday). Make up any other information you think you need.

_____

_____

_____

_____

_____

_____

_____

_____

_____

_____

LESSON 7.6

Résumés

Objective   To write a résumé.

The two things you will most likely need to get a job are a job application and a résumé.

A job application could be a letter you write to an employer. It will probably be an application blank you fill in at the place of employment.

A résumé is like a portrait of you—it shows who you are with respect to your educational and work experience. You want your résumé to give an employer a true picture of who you are and what you can do. The common kind of résumé is a chronological one—in it, you highlight the most important facts in order of when they happened, starting from the most recent and going backward.

The following suggests items to include in a résumé. Read it through, and see what parts could be used in your résumé. A résumé is different for each person, but any résumé should be clear, concise, and neatly typed and copied on quality paper.

♦   A Chronological Résumé

YOUR NAME

Permanent Address:
Street Address
City, State Zip
Phone Number

Professional Objective:
State the type of position that you are applying for and your long-term goal. In your objective, you may include indications of wanting growth and challenge. Example: An entry-level job in data processing leading to a career in systems analysis.

Education:
List professional training and/or college(s) first and then high school attended, with date of graduation along with degree and major. List the most recent program first, and work backwards, in order.

Courses: (Optional)
List no more than six; list only those that have something to do with the position for which you are applying, and tell how they apply to the position.

Special Skills: (Optional)
List skills acquired through training or through your own initiative. They can be concrete (typing, shorthand, computer operations) or abstract (organizational, public speaking, management, etc.). Show diversity.

Work Experience:
List the most recent job first and work backwards in time. Include part-time and summer work. Give brief job descriptions and dates of employment. If your employment history includes many short-term, miscellaneous jobs, use the following rules:
1. List those relevant to the position for which you are applying.
2. List those you held for the longest periods of time.

Extracurricular Activities, Hobbies: (optional)
List any professional or community organizations individually, along with responsibilities you held. Then list hobbies and special interests that might be pertinent to the position for which you are applying. Also list others that seem less relevant if they will indicate your diversity in a variety of areas.

Personal Data: (Optional)
You may wish to note your general good health and marital and dependent status here. (Some employers may feel that a married person is more stable, while others might feel that a single person would be more suitable for a job requiring a lot of traveling. Your statement could be just ''Single, excellent health'').

References: (Optional)
List at least three, or state that they are available upon request. Be sure to get permission in advance from the people you wish to list. Teachers, friends, or former employers (do not use relatives) make good references. Include names, titles, addresses, and telephone numbers with area codes. Then ask your chosen references to send you a typed recommendation, or let the person know who might be calling them for a verbal recommendation. If you have written recommendations, make copies of them and have them ready to mail on request. You could also take them with you to an interview.

Now that you have looked over the list of suggestions, use this worksheet to make a rough draft of your résumé.

Resumé Worksheet

(Name) _____

(Permanent Address) _____

_____

_____

Professional Objective: *(or Career Goal)*

_____

_____

_____

Education:

_____ _____
(Date)   _____

_____ _____
(Date)   _____

Courses: *(Optional)*

_____

_____

Special Skills: *(Optional)*

_____

_____

Work Experience: *(or Employment History)*

_____ Company Name: _____
(Date)   Address: _____
                 Position: _____
                 Duties: _____
                 _____

_____ Company Name: _____
(Date)   Address: _____
                 Position: _____
                 Duties: _____
                 _____

_____ Company Name: _____
(Date)   Address: _____
                 Position: _____
                 Duties: _____
                 _____

_____ Company Name: _____
(Date)   Address: _____
                 Position: _____
                 Duties: _____
                 _____

Personal Data: *(Optional)*

References:

(If your work experience is more recent than your education, put it before "Education.")

Have a counselor or a professional person who is familiar with résumés read over your résumé. The counselor can give you his or her reaction to the résumé (Does it present a true and favorable picture of you? Would it make the person want to hire you?) and offer any suggestions he or she may have. Keep working on the résumé until it is the best you can make it.

Keep in mind that if you apply for different types of positions, you may need to have more than one résumé. The skills, training, and job experiences for one position might not be the most relevant for another position.

Remember that your résumé is often the first look at you that a prospective employer gets. Make it a good one.

Answer Key

Chapter 1

LESSON 1.1

1. conference, Canada
2. boss, memo, time
3. restaurant, tables, people, tables, people
4. Malcolm, hours, lunch
5. Sherry, receptionist, people
6. repairman, condenser, refrigerator
7. caterer, tablecloths
8. tourists, Mexico
9. judge, stenographer, statement
10. jobs, secretaries, Washington, D.C.

LESSON 1.2

1. hospitals
2. floors
3. pencils
4. pipes
5. orders
6. samples
7. monitors
8. invoices
9. jobs
10. technicians

11. pen
12. uniform
13. blank
14. call
15. machine
16. raise
17. sale
18. brake
19. computer
20. paper

21. clients
22. Sales
23. sample
24. floors
25. transmission
26. keyboard
27. shifts
28. idea
29. résumés
30. appointment

LESSON 1.3

1. replies
2. solos
3. leaves
4. commanders-in-chief
5. alloys
6. emergencies
7. bosses
8. finishes
9. cafés
10. stitches
11. series
12. dictionaries
13. certified public accountants
14. brain waves

15. waitresses
16. videos
17. boxes
18. repairmen
19. halves
20. data processors

LESSON 1.4

1. the computer's keyboard
2. Maria's secretary
3. the accountant's calculator
4. the welders' tools
5. the salespeople's samples
6. the chef's recipes
7. the nurse's uniform
8. the lab technician's reputation
9. the hotel's rooms
10. the administrator's assistant

11. ship's
12. doctor's
13. secretaries'
14. patients'
15. car's
16. printers'
17. plumber's
18. room's
19. building's
20. women's

LESSON 1.5

1. you, me
2. his, they, him
3. I, you, I
4. She, her
5. They, him, his
6. me, my
7. They, them
8. He, his, him
9. Our, theirs
10. We, their

LESSON 1.6

1. his, antecedent: Luis
2. her, antecedent: Cathy
3. he, antecedent: Tom
4. their, antecedent: them
5. your, antecedent: Vanessa or you
6. he, antecedent: Aaron
7. they, antecedent: staff
8. its, antecedent: shop
9. her, antecedent: Sandy
10. her, antecedent: Janelle

LESSON 1.7

1. works, A
2. needs, A
3. hired, A
4. asked, A
5. wrote, A
6. answered, A

7. became, B   8. is, B
9. drew, A   10. was, B

11. searched   12. Send
13. takes   14. shipped
15. is   16. made
17. refused   18. discussed
19. was   20. referred

LESSON 1.8

1. reserved, will reserve
2. fill, will fill
3. added, will add
4. order, ordered
5. attended, will attend
6. manage, will manage
7. weld, welded
8. checked, will check
9. maintain, maintained
10. processed, will process
11. examine, will examine
12. draft, will draft
13. clean, cleaned
14. filed, will file
15. mailed, will mail
16. count, will count
17. serve, served
18. cook, will cook
19. received, will receive
20. talk, will talk

LESSON 1.9

1. prescribing   prescribed   prescribed
2. removing   removed   removed
3. analyzing   analyzed   analyzed
4. purchasing   purchased   purchased
5. practicing   practiced   practiced
6. listening   listened   listened
7. responding   responded   responded
8. learning   learned   learned
9. decaying   decayed   decayed
10. establishing   established   established
11. discovering   discovered   discovered
12. typing   typed   typed
13. entering   entered   entered
14. calling   called   called
15. preparing   prepared   prepared

16.	cleaning	cleaned	cleaned
17.	storing	stored	stored
18.	working	worked	worked
19.	completing	completed	completed
20.	estimating	estimated	estimated

LESSON 1.10

1.	has/have purchased	had purchased	will have purchased
2.	has/have asked	had asked	will have asked
3.	has/have watched	had watched	will have watched
4.	has/have recorded	had recorded	will have recorded
5.	has/have employed	had employed	will have employed
6.	has/have used	had used	will have used
7.	has/have audited	had audited	will have audited
8.	has/have increased	had increased	will have increased
9.	has/have expressed	had expressed	will have expressed
10.	has/have defended	had defended	will have defended

11.	will have baked	12.	had formed
13.	have earned	14.	will have researched
15.	had repaired	16.	had typed
17.	has requested	18.	have ordered
19.	will have saved	20.	has promoted

LESSON 1.11

1.	he was interpreting	2.	he is occupying
3.	he will have been replacing	4.	he has been delaying
5.	he had been devising	6.	he will be monitoring
7.	he is producing	8.	he had been examining
9.	he will be managing	10.	he was ordering

11.	are	12.	will have been
13.	were	14.	has been
15.	will be	16.	had been
17.	will be	18.	are
19.	have been	20.	were

LESSON 1.12

1.	ran	2.	will have grown
3.	had taken	4.	have bought
5.	began	6.	has drawn
7.	had written	8.	will have read
9.	lent	10.	had paid
11.	met	12.	have bid
13.	will have had	14.	spoke
15.	have chosen	16.	will have cost

17. knew   18. will have taught
19. had forgotten 20. have dealt

LESSON 1.13

1. The, summer, the, new, fall
2. the, first, the
3. your, recent, good, white
4. The, dental, a, careful, complete, her
5. A, safety
6. A, computer-repair, many, special
7. The, auto-body, the, terrible, the, front
8. her, the, 6 o'clock
9. An, efficient, caring, nurse's, a, valuable
10. The, that, old

11. proper   12. article
13. descriptive   14. descriptive
15. compound   16. demonstrative
17. descriptive   18. descriptive
19. possessive   20. compound

LESSON 1.14

1. faster   fastest
2. more skillful   most skillful
3. stronger   strongest
4. more healthful   most healthful
5. later   latest
6. more valuable   most valuable
7. more intelligent   most intelligent
8. more sour   most sour
9. more careless   most careless
10. more self-confident most self-confident
11. better   best
12. more dangerous   most dangerous
13. more boring   most boring
14. tastier   tastiest
15. more talented   most talented
16. more popular   most popular
17. thinner   thinnest
18. more unhealthy   most unhealthy
19. sloppier   sloppiest
20. more efficient   most efficient

LESSON 1.15

1. newly, more
2. more, smoothly, before
3. loudly, most
4. quickly, carefully
5. well
6. thoroughly
7. more, efficiently
8. aggressively, very
9. badly, only
10. suddenly, off

11. proudly modifies told
13. gently modifies put
15. steadily modifies improved
17. distinctly and fast modify speaks
    not and too modify fast
19. always and early modify
    should arrive

12. very modifies skilled
14. often modifies calls
16. not modifies did mind
18. out and promptly modify
    should have gone
20. only modifies would speak

LESSON 1.16

1. at, of
2. at, on
3. in, from, until
4. on, next to
5. Throughout, beside
6. out of, for
7. on, of, instead of
8. as, in, outside of
9. Despite, in
10. concerning, by

11. Between you and me; objects: you, me
    since graduation; object: graduation
12. of the letter; object: letter
    under your paperweight; object: paperweight
13. on the wall; object: wall
    above the telephone; object: telephone
14. around the patient's neck; object: neck
15. until 5 P.M.; object: 5 P.M.
    of the week; object: week
16. toward which; object: which
17. of the union; object: union
    against longer workdays; object: workdays
18. during the holidays; object: holidays
19. for the banquet; object: banquet
    alongside the cheese; object: cheese
    behind the vegetables; object: vegetables
20. off my car; object: car
    after the accident; object: accident

LESSON 1.17

1. among
2. from
3. from
4. Besides
5. speak to
6. off
7. between
8. beside
9. into
10. speak with

11. This is the program about which she was talking.
12. When Paul had his car repainted, the color was very different from what he expected.
13. Besides plane reservations, the travel agent also made hotel reservations.
14. When the computer crashed, we had to borrow a backup disk from my brother.

15. The presentation at the dinner went very well because the slide projector was right beside the speakers' table.
16. After Marisol received her award, she stepped off the platform.
17. Speak with your supervisor about any schedule changes you might like.
18. To whom did you send invitations?
19. The catering director left to get a menu from the waitress.
20. Since Janelle was the newest employee, she could only choose between two vacation weeks.

LESSON 1.18

1. either . . . or, correlative
2. or, coordinating
3. so, coordinating
4. both . . . and, correlative
5. not only . . . but also, correlative
6. Just as . . . so, correlative
7. and, coordinating
8. Neither . . . nor, correlative
9. Whether . . . or, correlative
10. but, coordinating

11. brushing, flossing
12. Boston, Washington, D.C.
13. Frank thought of being an auto mechanic, he became a welder instead
14. today, tomorrow
15. Anne, assistant
16. Mr. Murphy needed to be in Chicago that day, he decided to fly
17. banks, credit unions
18. hundreds of our students have gotten good jobs after graduation, can you
19. in color, in black and white
20. a legal, a medical

LESSON 1.19

1. Quiet!
2. Help!
3. Oh
4. Well
5. Hey!
6. Hooray!
7. Well!
8. Congratulations!
9. Wow!
10. Sorry

11–15 Answers will vary; the following are suggestions:

11. Great!
12. Well
13. My goodness!
14. Ouch!
15. Help!

Chapter 2

LESSON 2.1

1. Yes
2. Yes
3. No
4. No
5. No
6. Yes

7. Yes   **8.** No
9. Yes   **10.** No

11. repairperson, advised
12. hotels, use
13. Mrs. Clarke, bought
14. Robots, can increase
15. Maria, types
16. account, called . . . advised
17. He, is studying
18. Michael . . . Luis received
19. professional, should add
20. states, have

LESSON 2.2

1. interrogative   **2.** declarative
3. imperative   **4.** interrogative
5. exclamatory   **6.** imperative
7. exclamatory   **8.** declarative
9. imperative   **10.** declarative

11. Robots can increase job safety by performing jobs that are dangerous for humans.
12. Is a service contract a good buy?
13. A salesperson usually gets a discount on any purchase where he or she works.
14. What a lovely display that is!
15. Fill out the application and sign it.
16. Does your business use seasonal workers?
17. How steadily you hold those instruments!
18. All the words in three average novels can be put on one floppy disk.
19. How cold should the inside of a good freezer be?
20. Please show me detailed drawings of your idea.

LESSON 2.3

1. buys, tools
2. wants, job
3. send, catalogs
4. Keep, receipts
5. helped, patient
6. reserved, seats
7. replaced, door
8. prepared, Anton
9. needed, samples
10. slid, disk

11. mailed, customers
12. offered, Shane
13. gave, instructor

14. saves, boss
15. sent, office
16. handed, Mrs. Rather
17. showed, Nelson
18. tossed, Sarah
19. read, boss
20. found, Jerome

LESSON 2.4

1. A   2. L
3. A   4. A
5. L   6. L
7. L   8. A
9. L   10. L

11. person, I	12. co-workers, They
13. bad, Mr. Fritz	14. doubtful, teller
15. powerful, air conditioner	16. smaller, house
17. afraid, Dolores	18. better, room
19. smaller, Profits	20. fine, engine

LESSON 2.5

1. us, objective	2. me, objective
3. them, objective	4. she, nominative
5. me, objective	6. I, nominative
7. she, nominative	8. my, possessive
9. she-I, nominative	10. We, nominative

LESSON 2.6

1. gerund phrase	2. infinitive phrase
3. participial phrase	4. prepositional phrase
5. gerund phrase	6. participial phrase
7. infinitive phrase	8. prepositional phrase
9. infinitive phrase	10. prepositional phrase

11. Left in charge of the display booth
12. Repairing the transmission
13. To learn computer programming
14. under the sink
15. listening to the radio
16. to finish the job today
17. to submit a bid
18. Learning shorthand
19. above the "shift" key
20. selling the most ads

LESSON 2.7

1.	Dependent	2.	Dependent
3.	Independent	4.	Independent
5.	Dependent	6.	Independent
7.	Dependent	8.	Independent
9.	Dependent	10.	Independent

11. Jean flew to the conference so she would have more time in New York.
12. Before Fred became a motorcycle technician, he was a motorcycle sales-man.
13. My office bought a new copy machine so we could process forms more quickly.
14. Although insurance is a big business, we try to keep our services on a personal level.
15. The secretary will send you your test results as soon as they come in.
16. Jackie had to redo the copies because they came out too light.
17. Unless you place your order eight weeks in advance, we cannot guarantee delivery.
18. Chris became a welder, for he likes working with his hands.
19. Kate is taking a vacation after she graduates from secretarial school.
20. As long as you make your payments on time, you will have a good credit rating.

Chapter 3

LESSON 3.1

1.	test	2.	run
3.	hires	4.	treat
5.	pay	6.	go
7.	program	8.	repairs
9.	types	10.	choose
11.	is	12.	are
13.	has	14.	work
15.	take	16.	covers
17.	were	18.	pay
19.	has	20.	are

LESSON 3.2

1.	contract!	2.	Friday?
3.	order.	4.	test.
5.	IRS?	6.	it!
7.	disk?	8.	COBOL.
9.	elevator.	10.	work.

11. Tiffany, Jed, and Allen work on the fourth floor.
12. No, that is not what I ordered.
13. Before you turn off the computer, remove the disk from the disk drive.
14. In that catalog, the price was $4.94 a dozen.
15. My brother is an orderly, and I am a nurse's aide.
16. That fender will have to be sanded, primed, and then painted.
17. Instead of dinner, would you like to have lunch?
18. After I finish with the doctor, I would like to make an appointment to have my teeth cleaned.
19. My car, unfortunately, needs a new muffler.
20. Your income taxes, of course, depend on how much you earn.
21. colon after ''cold''
22. semicolon after ''résumé''
23. colon after ''benefits''
24. semicolon after ''week''
25. colon after ''fat''

26. (Monday through Friday).
27. two-week
28. When you are ready—and I hope it's soon—you can finish that typing.
29. (men and women)
30. family-oriented

LESSON 3.3

There may be some variation in the following sentences:

1. Miguel saw his lunch in the refrigerator.
2. Desirous of avoiding a strike, the negotiating committee drew up a new union contract.
3. The computer, its monitor, and the printer cost a total of $2,000.
4. On your way out, be sure to put that letter in the IN box.
5. While I was driving to work, my car had a flat tire.
6. While Rosa was at lunch, her patient, Mrs. Amano, had X rays taken.
7. After you type a letter, your boss should check it for errors.
8. The doctor told Anne to stay in bed three days because she was recovering from the flu.
9. The operator's manual seems to show that the start button is the red one.
10. The pharmacist asked Mario to lock the drugstore every night during his, the pharmacist's, vacation.

LESSON 3.4

1. computer programming
2. a one-room efficiency
3. Senator Jones
4. *Career Options*
5. Angela McGuinness
6. Sherry
7. Friday
8. Sam Cooper
9. the gray pinstripe
10. Randy

11. Commas around Wayne Chong because most people only have one boss—the meaning would still be clear without "Wayne Chong."
12. No commas around Rob because most people have more than one friend.
13. Commas around Ms. Nunes because there is only one head teller.
14. Commas around *Repairing Your Own Computer* because there can only be one first book.
15. No commas around Nicole because there are two sisters and the sentence needs to specify which sister.

16. Brian's hobby, fixing old radios, became his career.
17. The dental assistant, Shelley Rogers, does not work on Tuesday.
18. The last day for submitting next year's budget is tomorrow, Thursday.
19. My favorite typist, Brandy, is leaving for another job.
20. That computer monitor, a color monitor, is out for servicing.

LESSON 3.5

1. "Are you familiar with this model refrigerator, Dion?" asked Mr. Fortin.
2. Mai, I need this finished by 3 o'clock.
3. When you are ready to start painting the pickup, Fabin, check with me about the color.
4. Mrs. Yarina said to me, "When the service rep shows up, Carol, send him to my office."
5. Bite down on the film, Will, and I'll take the X ray.
6. I heard the traffic reporter say, "Avoid the Tenth Street Bridge because of roadwork."
7. "That estimate," she said, "is much too high."
8. "Ladies and gentlemen, we have a new supervisor," he announced.
9. "Stand when the judge comes in," the lawyer whispered to his client.
10. The nurse promised, "This won't hurt."

Chapter 4

LESSON 4.1

1. Senior citizens don't have to run marathons to reap the benefits of physical fitness.
2. Always keep the recommended tire pressure in all your tires, including the spare.
3. There are few things that you touch or depend upon during the day that haven't been made by welding.
4. Ordinary, everyday contact will not give you AIDS.
5. But research began in the early 1970s has proven that pets promote both physical and mental well-being.

LESSON 4.2

1. The capitol of Maryland is Annapolis.
2. And a new tire is expensive.

3. One of the most popular singing groups is the Beatles.
4. People have fun at DisneyWorld, too.
5. People in Europe usually learn to speak English in school.

There may be some variation in answers to 6–10.

6. But when you order your coffee, you clearly hear the voice of an almost unchanged region in your waitress's Cajun accent; * after "American scene."
7. Many older Americans are seriously malnourished; * at beginning of paragraph.
8. In moments, they are airborne, en route to Guaymas, Mexico, on the first leg of the monthly trip with Liga; * should be at end of paragraph.
9. The dentist made a thorough examination; * should be after "the nearest dentist."
10. The responsibility belonged to the teller, not the tool; * should be at the end of the paragraph.

LESSON 4.3

1. How-to paragraph
2. Contrasting paragraph
3. Persuasive paragraph
4. Descriptive paragraph
5. Cause-and-effect paragraph

LESSON 4.4

The linking words are listed in order from the beginning of the paragraph.

1. still, For example, In addition, while, Finally, until, As a result
2. In spite of, But, More and more, though, however, Without doubt

Answers 3–7 can vary. The following are suggestions:

3. So   4. Since
5. Even so   6. As soon as
7. In spite of

Chapter 5

LESSON 5.1

The verbs are given in order:

1. advised, will be, thinks, beams
2. has returned, reopened, contains, was turned, will be

LESSON 5.2

1. third
2. first

3. second
4. first
5. second
6. third
7. first
8. second
9. first
10. second

11. Answers will vary, but should be something like the following:

Memo to the Staff
    Many of you know Betty Jonas. She has been a valued employee in the shipping department for 43 years. On June 30, Betty will retire from our company. We will miss her and hope she enjoys a comfortable retirement.

12. Answers will vary, but should be something like the following:

Ace Accounting is pleased to announce the relocation of its offices from its present address, 692 Washington Street, to the Star Building at 250 Industrial Boulevard. The new quarters will house the newly expanded staff and allow for the parking of 100 cars and the company share vans. The move will be complete on September 1.

LESSON 5.3

1. Inconsistent—Stephanie bought a new computer. She paid $1,500 for it.
2. Consistent
3. Inconsistent—The dentist and the technician both told me I should floss more often. They told me to use unwaxed dental floss.
4. Consistent
5. Consistent
6. Inconsistent—Dimiso had his computer memory upgraded to 8K. He hopes it will meet his needs.
7. Inconsistent—The secretary wrote my name in the appointment book, but he/she forgot to give me a card.
8. Consistent
9. Inconsistent—Leroy reread the statement of the witness to the judge. He has a loud, clear voice.
10. Inconsistent—Julio and Melti are home health-care aides. They each have about 10 patients a day.

LESSON 5.4

1. active   2. active
3. active   4. passive
5. passive   6. active

7. passive   **8.** active
9. passive   **10.** active

Answers will vary. The following are suggestions:

11. Sando changes the computer ribbon about twice a month.
12. Every company at the job fair held interviews.
13. Trevor's company copied and bound the reports.
14. You should change your car's oil every 3,000 miles.
15. The medical assistant took the blood samples for five tests.

LESSON 5.5

Answers will vary. The following are suggestions:

1. A boss should value a secretary's work.
2. The electricians in my company are thinking of forming a group called United Electricians.
3. Nurse's aides must buy their own uniforms.
4. A computer repairperson earns good money.
5. A dental technician wears rubber gloves when cleaning a patient's teeth.
6. A career in welding would be a good choice for anyone who likes working with his or her hands (OR who likes manual work; OR for people who like working with their hands).
7. A food-service worker in a school must start the day very early.
8. The legal assistant read the notes to the lawyer.
9. A travel agent tries to get the best rates available for customers.
10. A salesperson looks forward to receiving a commission on sales.

LESSON 5.6

1. The top (three) sales(men) for the month (is) Anna Alvarez and Todd Wilkins. These people had sales over $10,000 each. Management is proud of them for helping (us) pass the goal of $100,000. (We) hope (you) (did) as well next (week)

Answers may vary. The following paragraph is one possibility:

The top two salespeople for the month are Anna Alvarez and Todd Wilkins. These people had sales over $10,000 each. We in management are proud of them for helping us pass the goal of $100,000. We hope they do as well next month.

2. Answers will vary. The following is one possibility:

Leroy is a bookkeeper who works for Best Manufacturing. Best Manufacturing is a small company that makes all kinds of screws, nuts, and bolts, which are shipped all over the world. About 75 people work in the shipping, order, bookkeeping, manufacturing, and design departments. Leroy's department has only four bookkeepers, but that is enough. Best Manufacturing is a nice company for which to work.

3. Answers will vary.

Chapter 6

LESSON 6.1

1. monitor	**9.** embarrass	**17.** unconscious
2. receive	**10.** sincerely	**18.** maintenance
3. foreign	**11.** dictation	**19.** conference
4. height	**12.** built	**20.** technician
5. section	**13.** association	**21.** sterilize
6. merge	**14.** guarantee	**22.** salaries
7. freight	**15.** strength	**23.** prepared
8. chronic	**16.** Wednesday	**24.** typing
		25. skimming

LESSON 6.2

1. straight	**9.** some	**17.** set
2. between	**10.** sure	**18.** like
3. very	**11.** your	**19.** stationery
4. lie	**12.** let, leave	**20.** almost
5. formerly	**13.** course	**21.** Whose
6. hiring, teach	**14.** than	**22.** lay
7. Can	**15.** Besides	**23.** guessed
8. They're	**16.** fourth	**24.** into
		25. may

LESSON 6.3

1. I work in the seagram's building on park avenue.

2. our fiscal year begins on july 1.

3. the first typewriter was manufactured by e. remington and sons.

4. sid is an assistant to an occupational therapist at saint joseph's hospital.

5. the computer came with a book titled *getting to know your computer*.

6. new year's day is a national holiday in the united states.

7. mrs. boudreau comes to collect the rent on the first thursday of the month.

8. <u>d</u>o you prefer <u>a</u>pple, <u>ibm</u>, or <u>h</u>ewlitt-<u>p</u>ackard computers?

9. <u>t</u>he contributions of workers are recognized on <u>l</u>abor <u>d</u>ay, the first <u>m</u>onday in <u>s</u>eptember in the <u>u</u>nited <u>s</u>tates and <u>c</u>anada.

10. <u>b</u>rian <u>c</u>larkson replaced <u>p</u>resident <u>s</u>tein as head of our firm.

11. *Roger A̶nd Me* is an interesting D̶ocumentary about working people.

12. Both M̶en and W̶omen have to take exams for C̶ivil S̶ervice jobs.

13. The B̶ank is open until 8:00 P.M. on Thursday and F̶RIDAY evenings.

14. My mother went to N̶ight S̶chool to learn S̶ecretarial skills.

15. When Roxy becomes a N̶urse's A̶ide, S̶he is moving to the C̶ity of Philadelphia.

LESSON 6.4

1. When the supplier calls⊙ please let me know⊙
   When the supplier calls, please let me know.

2. Jamal⊙you should be in court July 12⊙ at 10 in the morning⊙
   Jamal, you should be in court July 12 at 10 in the morning.

3. Mr⊙ Whitfield called and said⊙ You have the job⊙
   Mr. Whitfield called and said, "You have the job."

4. The meeting in Chicago⊙ Illinois⊙ is taking place on Monday⊙Tuesday⊙ and Wednesday⊙
   The meeting in Chicago, Illinois, is taking place on Monday, Tuesday, and Wednesday.

5. My partner ⊙Andy Maciel⊙ gave Mrs⊙Quinn the estimate ⊖ to fix her bumper⊙
   My partner, Andy Maciel, gave Mrs. Quinn the estimate to fix her bumper.

6. At People's Bank in Bridgeport⌃Connecticut⌃employees view a video showing an angry customer talking to a teller. Then the employees discuss what might have occurred in the customer's day before the visit to the bank⊙ "You cannot control events in your customer's day or your customer's feelings about the day⌃ says Carole Callahan⌃ manager of management development⊙ Employees learn self-management techniques⊙ Instead of blaming themselves when faced with an angry customer⌃ employees learn to remain calm⌃ to empathize⌃ and to ask themselves what they can do to improve the situation⌃ Callahan says⊙

LESSON 6.5

1. when a car is damaged in an accident it is taken to an auto-body shop for repairs.

2. A computer only works on the data it is given from a floppy disk or from a hard drive.

3. A bank offers such services as saving, lending, and checking.

4. if someone wants to be a nurse's aide that person should have an interest in medicine. THE person should also be able to follow orders exactly and like taking care of people.

5. A legal stenographer sits in a courtroom every day. he or she listens to every word that is said by witnesses, lawyers, and the judge and records it on a special typewriter.

Chapter 7

LESSON 7.1

1. Answers will vary. The addresses must be included in the correct form. The letter should be written in polite language, giving the correct message and information. The letter should end with the proper closing.
2. Answers will vary. The letter should be written in the correct form. It should state why the writer is answering the ad and why the person is qualified for the job.

LESSON 7.2

1. Answers will vary. Since the situation is rather informal, the tone of the memo can be informal. The most important thing is that the information be accurate and complete.
2. Answers will vary. This memo should be more formal than the picnic memo and very briefly give the necessary facts.
3. Answers will vary. A reminder memo is very short, often on a form notice, with just the appointment information. It should mention the name of the dentist in case the patient deals with more than one dentist.
4. Answers will vary. This memo is like a short letter and must contain whatever information the personnel department will need to know to select an appropriate bookkeeper.

LESSON 7.3

1. Wording can vary somewhat. The invitation must be written in the third person and should follow the form of the sample given in the lesson.
2. Answers will vary. The tone will be informal and should include date, time, and place.
3. Wording can vary somewhat. The ''card'' should be correctly filled in with all the necessary information.

LESSON 7.4

1. Answers will vary. All blanks should be filled in clearly and the appropriate boxes marked off.
2. Answers will vary. All appropriate blanks should be filled in clearly and boxes marked off.
3. Answers will vary. Notice that this form says ''print.'' Be sure the money blanks are handled correctly.
4. Answers will vary. It is important that all areas are filled in in some way.
5. Answers will vary.
6. Answers will vary.

LESSON 7.5

1. Wording can vary. You should make up information for these blanks: To, Date, and Time. Check off the boxes by TELEPHONED and PLEASE CALL. The message should be clearly written.
2. Wording can vary. You have the name for ''To'' and the message. Make up the date and time. Assume that Jason Bedard's mother's name is Mrs. Bedard, but that might not be true if she has been married more than once or uses her maiden name. Just ignore the ''M'' and put ''your mother'' in the blank. The information does not say that Jason should call back, so just TELEPHONED should be checked off. You can make up the mother's telephone number or assume that Jason knows his mother's telephone number.
3. Wording will vary. This message will read like a memo and should contain the same type of information that appears on the ''WHILE YOU WERE OUT'' form.

LESSON 7.6

Be aware that a résumé is something that goes through several drafts and rewritings. You should use this form for your rough draft and type up a current and professional-looking résumé when you begin job hunting.

Index